The Tallest Mountain Series BOOK ONE

Get
Yourself
UP

Motivation and Inspiration
To Keep Pressing Forward
For the Next Generation

ALMA L. CARR-JONES

Published by TMP Books, 3 Central Plaza Ste 307, Rome, GA 30161

www.TMPBooks.com

Dedicated to

Mrs. **Lula Mae Peters–Carr**, My Momma

"The Preacher's Daughter"

I am just a country bumpkin
Still holding on to the standards
With which I was raised
For my Momma, a preacher's daughter
Was a godly woman, the Lord be praised.
Since my Momma was a preacher's daughter
There were certain things that she did not condone
And would not allow her children to do
For when we did she would give us a look
That would chill us to the bone.
I remember what you taught me, Momma
And always strive to do the things that I know
Would make you proud of me each day
By living for the Lord and being an
Example of love along the way.
With Love,
Alma

To Owen and Royal

To the God of Heaven by Which I Can Tell the World
DEI Sub Numine Viget
(Under Your Spirit, I Flourish)

Acknowledgements and Thanks

I want to extend grateful thanks to the ladies who demanded I write this book, the second in my inspirational series for women. May it be a blessing to you as well as others.

To My Readers
I talked to the Lord about you
Just a little while ago
I thanked Him for your being
A part of my readership
And asked Him to bless you …
I thought you'd like to know.
Alma

My *Love for God and His love for me is not my best*
Kept secret as a Christian because He gave His
Love to me for me to give it away
And to keep giving and giving even
After my body has gone back to the clay.

TABLE OF CONTENTS

Introduction 3

LESSON 1 13

LESSON 2 41

LESSON 3 99

LESSON 4 137

About the Author... 193

Other Books by the Author 194

Introduction

God is great, and I know most of you already know that. He is great in everything He does. But I wanted to make it personal today.

My Reason for Living

I live my life – for Him

Every breath I breathe, I breathe – for Him

Why? He gave His life to save me

The least that I can do is live – for Him

Which means that encouraging you, inspiring

You and or making you laugh are

All done in service and to show my love – for Him

Thus my reason for giving.

****

My purpose for this book is threefold:

1. To inform people of the awesome responsibility we have in the preparation and instruction of future generations — *With the advancement of age comes the realization of the importance of preparation of self and of others. Things that once commanded our attention have taken a backseat to the things that have been the most important, all along.*

2. To encourage children and adults alike with incidents from the Holy Writ and from my life about the love of the Lord and His care for all and His ever-ready availability to us, if we but listen — *Having done a blog on the need for children to be instructed in the desirable way we want them to go, a reader of mine commented about how much of our cultural good points have been lost and she was correct. But we can stop the loss and start to build it back.*

3. To leave words for the future church to have on hand as they make their way in this world because sometimes it helps to recall those conversations you had with wise loved ones who have gone on. But there are so many folks who may not have given heed to, or ever had the opportunity to sit under the tutelage of a wise one — *While some of us have been aware, all along, of what is most important on this journey of ours, the passage of time causes us to be more vocal and to leave no stone unturned in our work for the Lord. For this generation and the next ones, we can write down sayings and words of old that have stood us in good stead in our lives. We need to keep a running record of what we have garnered in our walk in this life and share it for all the world to share with their posterity.*

Writing It Down

Writing speaks to my soul
Brings me joy
Makes my heart sing
And makes my bells of contentment ring
As encouraging and inspiring words
To mine and other's posterity, I bring.

****

My writing is my way of saying to the Lord, "Thanks for my journey." Deciding to write almost exclusively for the Lord God has made me introspective and has been a profound heart-touching, enlightening experience. There is within me a "fire that rages through my bones," as Jeremiah said.

For You

It is my hope that the lessons, stories (cases in point), poems, and essays I have written bring you encouragement, peace, and joy as I praise my God in His glory by telling my story.

As I said, it is my intent to encourage you by loving you with words as I remind you of the great love we have in our God! I found something good, and I want to share Him with you. Those of us who already know Him realize the difference He makes in our lives, so we rejoice already. Those of you who don't, this is an opportunity to get to know Him. He is like a fresh drink of water from an oasis that you come across in the desert. One drink and you will hunger for Him. That, my friend, is unmitigated joy. You will never let Him go, and you will wonder how you made it this long without an intimate relationship with Him. If I sound grateful, it is because I am. He means the world to me, and I will proclaim it however I can, wherever I go.

I mean, He is so great at what He does as can be seen by His creation of the world and His creation of man. He knows everything about everything that is and that will be. I am glad that when He was taking stock of what He had created in mankind, He did not stop when it came to me. The number of the hairs on my head were counted, too, as were yours. I am so glad He did not run out of patience when He came to this little vessel of clay named Alma. He did not run out of lovingkindness, justice, or righteousness. And I am so thankful He took the time to measure in a little more grace and mercy. I am glad and thankful He took the time to fashion me as He did and put a desire in me to serve Him. And I am glad He remembered that desire when I was a child and that He remembers it still.

But you know, when I asked the Lord to use me in His service, I never imagined in my wildest dreams that one day I would be writing a blog and subsequent books that would reach around the world! Yes, I told Him in a moment of prayerful adoration and fervor that I loved Him so much that I would stand on top of the tallest mountain in the world and shout my love for Him. I meant it then and still do now. I am just awestruck somewhat today when I begin to realize the magnitude of the blessing that He has afforded me.

Josh Groban's song, "You Raise Me Up" resonates so personally with me. Listen to the words on YouTube and see if it resonates with you, too: https://youtu.be/aJxrX42WcjQ.

In Short

God is the only reason I made it this far. So, I stand on top of the tallest mountain in my world yelling:

"I know that God answers prayer and will provide!"

Y'all, I read about how the Bible says He is faithful, but through the process of living life, my soul can testify and say, "I know that He is faithful." I am so glad that in all He does, He continues to remember even me.

A Poem of Praise
You have allowed me to be
You, my God, are the reason
That I can have joy in the midst of pain
You are why I can sing
Though walking through the rain
You are why I find joy in life
No matter what the season
You, my God, my Father, my Friend
Have allowed this earthen vessel to just be
And I, oh Lord, will proclaim Your Majestic grace
Before all humanity
For You have taught me, with patience
All the things I needed to learn
YOU, MY FATHER, ARE MY BLESSING
Through Jesus and the Holy Spirit
And I am proud to tell the world about it.
As I said, folks, sometimes nothing
But a praise poem or prayer will satisfy the yearning
And longing that drives me to seek His throne
As my faltering footsteps make their way home.

****

So please join me in a prayer of thanksgiving to Him.

Father, the Creator of all things, I want to say, "Thank You." Thanks to You for every blessing, mountain, hill, and storm that I have had in my life. Thank You for giving me the understanding that when You said You were faithful, You were really telling me You would never leave me floundering in this world alone. Thank You for the patience in teaching me that. Thank You for extending the hospitality and availability of Your throne to me. Thank You for allowing even me to serve You. Thank You for continuing to remember that I am but dust. In the name of Jesus, Amen.

It's a Wrap

History says that several hundred years ago when there was important news to be shared that people would go around ringing a bell and spreading the news. So, I will use a play on words and in a like manner, spread my news. What news? The news of my praise for Him and my faith, of course. So, in keeping with that, I wanted to share with you a poem of mine, "My Faith Bell." This poem is formatted as shape poetry. The poem is crafted to look like one of those old–fashioned hand rung bells. I have already told you that I told God one morning in prayer that if He put me on the top of the tallest mountain in the world, I would still be up there shouting my love for Him and talking about His love for mankind. Having said that, I hope you will enjoy this poem, which rings my message out loudly and clearly.

My
Faith
B
e
l
l

Faith began building in me a long time ago
By my Momma telling me of the God that she did know
Because she was so happy when she explained her faith in God
I decided that I would like this God to be my Friend, too
So began my walk of faith, now I am talking about Him to you
Because He has been with me wherever my footsteps have trod
And I am thankful for the day that my Momma
Talked to me about her God.
You will be too
When your
Children
Spout
Love
For
Him
As
We
Are
Prone
To do
!

So, folks, let's ring our bell and ring it loud and long, so people will want to know what all the noise is about as we tell them about our not–so–best–kept secret of the sheer joy of working for our God!

Swing that bell with a stroke that is good and strong
Because one day we will be telling our story among Heaven's
throng!

****

~From a speck of dust to the Creator of us all~

Preface

God has done it, y'all, and my cup runs over with the need to tell my story about His lovingkindness, justice, and righteousness! Today, I present to you ***The Tallest Mountain in My World Inspirational Series***. The title you see is one that came to me in a moment of early morning prayer.

I do love writing inspirational pieces for you, my friend. As always, I ask for your prayers of goodwill and accomplishment with this new book and all that it entails.

Musings from a Kept Child Who Keeps on Keeping on

When folk and situations didn't turn out the way I thought they would, God kept me and He's keeping me still. When disappointment threatened to take me down, God kept me and is keeping me still. When diabetes invaded my body, He kept me and is keeping me still. When I thought I was in the know in a given situation and it turned out I was on the outside and didn't know anything, He kept me and is keeping me still.

Forty years ago, when I left Old Fulton Road to go on the ministerial field with my husband, I had stars in my eyes and relatively few bruises. Oh, but now… that is why I can say to you, not only did God keep me, but He kept me in a big way, and is keeping me still.

So, if you know, like me, how valuable a relationship with God is, then you ought to tell somebody because our world is hurting for lack of knowledge of God and His love for mankind.

–As always, my writing is from my heart to yours.

Lesson 1:

As a Child

Scripture: 2 Timothy 1:5, 2 Timothy 3:14–15

Aim: TO LEARN THE IMPORTANCE of outfitting our children with a sure foundation by taking a retrospective look at our own lives. TO REALIZE THAT we are special and to recognize the necessity of teaching our children that fact.

Song: Yes, Jesus Loves Me

My Momma has passed on to the other side, but she left me some valuable assets. She left me with a love for people and a love for the Lord. That is one of the reasons I share my inspirational thoughts with you. Another reason is because that's the way I am made, meaning it must be what God intended.

I have always been one of those people who shared any lesson I learned with others. I learned early on in life that if something confused me it probably confused at least one other person. You remember how some of us used to be. We would be sitting in a learning situation of some sort or another and would not ask a question because we did not want to feel uninformed or "look dumb." Y'all know what I am talking about.

I realize anything that the Lord allows me to learn is for the good of myself and for the good of my fellowman. Therefore, I share through my writing, my books, and my speaking.

As I meditate each morning and as I live each day, my mind is like a sponge soaking up lessons to use for my writing. If something astounds me, then in some way it will sooner or later be featured in my writing, whether blog or book.

Looking back down through the years I can see that in His plan for my life, God made provision for me to be able to use the wisdom I asked for as a child in doing the jobs I would be given to do for Him over the course of my life. He began developing that wisdom in me at a young age.

I am going to use an incident in my life as a case in point for Lessons 1 and 2 in this book. Walk with me down the memory pages of my mind as I give you a little bit of my early life.

As I begin my perusal of my first memories, those of myself as a toddler, I trust you will be helped by its telling.

Life for me was pretty routine for a little one who was the only girl and the apple of her daddy's eye. I remember some things that happened, even at that age. My mother often exclaimed to me in later years that I couldn't remember certain things because I was just too little at the time they happened! She said that it just was not possible.

Case in Point – But I Do Remember

Here is one incident I remember, and I am thankful God did not allow it to color my childhood in a bad way. I remember one day my Momma's showing me my daddy going into the back door of a house down the road. I remember the resulting row that followed when he did come home. *(I was only a year and nine months old at the time. Nevertheless, I remember. That is why I tell you folks, you must be careful what young ones are exposed to because they can form memories, the weight of which, they can carry a lifetime. Fortunately, I was able to color the incident under Momma's favorite words, "That's just the way it is.")* I didn't know it then, but those words were to carry me through my entire lifetime, pretty much. They carried me through my daddy never coming back (when he did leave), the rough days of want during my growing up years, my Momma's passing, my house fire, and more.

At any rate, I digress, the row. I remember running to the house across the dirt road that had a dirt floor, screaming because I thought daddy was going to kill Momma. (Of course, he wasn't, he just took the axe away from her.) And yes, I remember my daddy raising his fist in a threatening motion to stop my brothers from crying and screaming because "Daddy was fighting Momma." I remember my Daddy picking me up and shushing me gently to quieten my sobs and eventually to stop my crying. I remember thinking, even back then, that my brothers had to be quiet and stop crying because Daddy had raised his fist to them, but not to me. He had picked me up and shushed and petted me like he always did.

"Nobody, but nobody better not make me cry 'cause my daddy would get 'em." My daddy would come unglued if I even whimpered. *(Yes, I can see now, that I was a **"thinking little thing" even way back then**. And I probably would have been spoiled rotten if Momma and daddy had stayed together, but they didn't, alas.) (Continued in Lesson 2 Case in Point)*

So, during my growing up years, this *thinking little thing*, instead, learned to put my brain on problems Momma had, and to try to help her figure things out. I remember the first time I tried to help her think about a problem she was worrying over and she told me that I was a child and to stay out of grown folks' business.

I remember hearing her hum. She had a certain tune she hummed when she was worried. I got pretty good at figuring out what was bothering her, too. And I remember thinking, "Why does she have to worry when I have an answer inside of me, but she won't listen because she thinks I am a child." I remember thinking that though I was a child, I thought like an adult. (Old folks back then used to tell me I was an "old soul." They said it so much I started to think that I was special. What they recognized in me was the placement of the wisdom I had asked God for every day as a child. Of course, I didn't realize it fully when I was a little girl. That would come years later.)

I remember one time in particular when Momma was worried, and I thought about how I could tell her that I had a suggestion about what she should do, but I had to figure out a way to tell her without, as she would say, "Getting out of a child's place."

I was in a dilemma, y'all, because I wanted to help her, but I did not want to get the legendary licks that would come if she thought I was being grown. So, here is what I did. I said, "Mommu–uh? Ain't trying to get out of a child's place or nothing, but I know what I would do if I had that problem." Momma sarcastically said, "And just what would you do, Miss Smarty?" I told her what I thought was a solution and it worked! She got to where she would often ask me what I thought about certain things and I would tell her.

Years later she would laugh and tell me, "Child, when you "squinched" those eyes together like that, I knew to get ready because a loo–loo was coming! Umph, Umph, Umph!

Something's been trying to get your attention all your life. Umph, Umph, Umph!" Then she would look at me like I had grown another head or something. Ha, ha. We laughed about my *strangeness* then.

Work in the Vineyard Is Almost Done, But I Learned

Yes, God has been with me through the years by making sure I learned positive long–lasting lessons from the things that happened in my life. And best of all, He made provision for me to feel useful even in my retirement years in that, I am using the story writing skills He allowed me to develop as a child to keep me busy. Yes, He allows me to help my fellowman with words that will comfort, inspire, and encourage now, and even after I am gone, and I am grateful for the job. I am going to share six specific lessons in this section of the book that I call ***The Practical.***

The Practical

Practical #1: *Using What You Have*

> $35 dollars a week is not very much
> That is what the lady lived on
> And she took care of three kids, with such
> Meager earnings as this –
> Life in her household was anything but bliss.

I think back at various times in my life and I see where I get my resilience from and my perseverance. Look at the lessons the Lord allowed me to learn about perseverance, resilience, and practicality through my Momma:

After she and my daddy separated, not having money to buy me new clothes, she made most of mine from material she found on the piece goods table at the dry goods store. She also cut down to fit me some of her old dresses that her boss lady had given her.

The same practicality was used in providing me with slips. She made them from the twenty-five-pound flour sacks that she bought flour in. She dumped the flour up in a lard can and voilà, she had material to make me a slip.

We had a container for meal as well. We did not keep meal in as large a quantity because sometimes the meal would go bad and have those little black bugs crawling in it; weevils, I think. Anyway, that batch had to be used. I just had to sift the weevils out and keep stepping.

Fatback was bought for frying as breakfast meat and as boiling meat for seasoning the dried beans we would have nearly every day. The fatback had to be boiled first to rid it of the excess salt it was packed in. Then that water was poured off and it was fried. Oh, such popping there was as the last of the water was fried off the fatback. When the fatback was fried, it tasted just like the chicharrons you can buy in packages in the potato chip aisle at the grocery store. Yum, yum, such good crunching there was! I never really cared for the boiled fatback though, so I would cut the skin off and eat that. It was quite tasty, too.

Momma never wasted anything. She used everything until it was used up.

Practical #2. *Don't Forget*

Every godly mother whether she is on this side or on the other side, wants her children to be faithful to God.

Remember when you ran carefree with total abandon and fell or was pushed and ended up with skinned knees? Remember how she chided you gently as she wiped your tears and lovingly tended your knees, "I told you to not run so fast," or "I told you not to run on those rocks. I told you to not play so roughly." You see, each of us will need to have the love of God to hold us and sustain us at some point in life (the times when life gives us scraped or skinned knees). Your mother knew that and knew she was giving you the most precious gift she could ever give you as her child, the Lord God. She knew she was giving you a garden to walk in when her days of walking with you were over.

Skinned Knees
Momma, I skinned my knees again from
Being tossed to the ground
But just like I did as a child, I found
Solace in the arms of your words, Momma, which
Have proven to be so profound.
Because you taught me to read my Bible, I
Go there time and time again
And receive solace aplenty when
The words of the Lord wrap around
Me, weary and worn though I am
But when I pick the fruit of Psalms
Sweet peace is what I seize
And I find that I can continue on
In spite of my skinned knees.

My Momma told me when I was young to always keep my hand in Jesus' hand. She said, "Alma, this Christian race is hard to run but never forget to take Jesus with you everywhere you go."

Y'all, I heeded that advice and still do, to this day. Do you know why? He won't leave me alone, ever! He has proven Himself time and time again.

And that is why the Lord is my Hero. If my fingers get too careworn and cannot grip His hand anymore, He holds me fast anyway. I am so glad to know His strength begins when mine ends. Here is a little verse I whipped up today to say to Him and to the world, "God be thanked, You live."

Jesus, when I fell into the trap that was made for me
You came with me to break my fall, and I thank You
You used the debris of my broken faith that was in shards
Around me to build my foundation anew
And now like the phoenix, I rise just as You told me I would do
So, Lord, thank You for giving me a Momma
Who, though she is gone, taught me
To always stick with and believe in You
Because she knew that You would always bring me through.

My Point

Why did I tell you all this about my early life and growing up years in my Momma's household? It is simple really; we are leaving a legacy daily. Are we teaching our children how to make do? If you don't do anything but tell them stories of how it was done, do that. Because of my Momma's resilience, I am the queen of perseverance and optimism.

So teaching them is the thing to do,
Better yet, write it down and let
Them see you living it, too.
That is what I am doing. I am writing down how my Momma had

the grit, determination, and faith to keep going. And you know what? She got to accomplish her goal of seeing her daughter settled into a fine job as a teacher. She got the chance to see her dream realized through me, as well as make sure that I was able and would be able to stand on my own two feet, with the help of God, if my situation in life should change for whatever reason. *(We will talk more about change of station in life in Book 2 of this series.)*

The lessons I learned as a child I still use until this day. And I have shared my Momma's legacy with you for yours...

Practical #3. *Jesus Won't Leave Me*

Ever Since I Can Remember

As you know by now, I tend to wax sentimental from time to time. I heard a song today that resonated with my life's journey so much that I decided to write about the subject of the song. Some things I remember from the past were of relatively short duration when compared to the span of my life to date. Yet, there are others that have lasted my entire lifetime. I am going to mention three such *lasting–a–lifetime* happenings now.

First Such, *Lasting–a–Lifetime,* **Happening**

I remember my daddy and the way he picked me up and twirled me in the air. I remember the way he made sure I was taken care of. My daddy made me feel special, and I learned early on that if I even grunted, he would come running into the room ready to spank my brothers. As I told you at the beginning of this lesson, I would have turned out to be a spoiled brat if he had stayed in my life for very long, but that was not to be the case. He and my

Momma separated for the last time when I was five years old. And I went from being daddy's little baby to a cry baby.

Though he told me he loved me and made me feel special, my daddy didn't stay. *(Hold that thought.)*

Second Such, *Lasting–a–Lifetime,* Happening

But my Momma did for as long as she could, and I remember so many kind and loving but ***teachable moments*** with her. I remember when she started to impart her values to me when she sat me down and talked to me about situations in life including my daddy and his penchant for women. Though I had to be told, she glossed over it and let me form my own conclusions. His absence over the years told me all I needed to know and then some. And when I was in the third grade, she sat me down and gave me a gift that was to stand the test of time. She gave me Jesus. (We will talk more about Jesus in the Third *Lasting–a–Lifetime* Happening.) So, I doted on my Momma, because she loved me and did not leave me like daddy did.

She reared me and was with me my whole life except for a few years after I went off to school and later got married. But still, she was where I could get to her when I needed to feel special or needed to be accepted just as I was. I cannot tell you how many trips I made down Interstate 40 from Martin to Memphis to visit my Momma. I probably went home every two weeks or so. That continued until I moved her to the city where I lived. That way, I could see her daily. As a matter of fact, she stayed with me for several years.

But then one day, Momma had to go away. And she went to where I could not get to her. If I heard something funny, I could not pick up the phone laughingly and say, "Guess what, Momma?" When somebody hurt my feelings, I could not go to her house and tell her all about it and leave with some of her well–chosen words of wisdom under my belt. I was alone, and I was bereft.

My Momma, though she loved me, couldn't stay.

Third Such, *Lasting–a–Lifetime* Happening

Now that we have reached the third one, I will do as I told you and talk about Jesus. I will never forget the day my Momma gave me the gift of Jesus. Because she was such a gifted storyteller, she paused at all the right places, and she raised and hushed her voice at the right times. When she finished telling me the story of Jesus, I was enthralled and went off to contemplate about this new thing she had told me about, about prayer to Jesus.

Yes, this prayer was different from the Lord's Prayer we said every night before going to sleep. It was my very own talk with Jesus. I could talk to Him like I talked to my daddy and Jesus would listen. This prayer thing was a wonderful new toy, and I started praying right then. And folks I have been praying ever since.

I remember the talks I used to have with Him when I did not even know Who He was. Most toddlers have a special friend, and I did, too. After Momma told me about Him, I made the connection, and I felt special, and I still feel special today though in a different way. I feel privileged to serve the Creator of this world with what little I can contribute. I feel grateful that He gives me something to do as I grow to full maturity to be made into pure gold. (Lesson 4.) I have learned that no matter what happens in life, ***Jesus will not leave me alone. He won't go to a*** *place where I cannot reach Him.* He will never leave me, and because He won't ever leave me, I will stay where my Momma put me, and not leave Him either. No other help I know.

June 6, 2021

Ever Since I Can Remember

Ever since I can remember
He has held my hand
He held my hand and made me feel special
When my daddy walked away
He held my hand and comforted me, and He did again
When my Momma had to leave me one day
But before she left my Momma reminded me of how Jesus had
Carried me and had allowed me to see success on top of success
She reminded me that she had placed me in His arms
A long time ago and in His arms, I was to stay.
So, I hold on to Jesus because I know that He will come
To get me and take me back to glory one day
And let me see my Momma, that sweet lady
Who took a part of me when she passed away.
She told me that just like He took care of me in college,
Gave me children and my own home, He would
Take care of me after she was gone
She also told me that I would find strength
That heretofore I had never realized I owned.
Ever since I can remember, the words
That she told me about Jesus rang true and still do…
What are the words that resound in your children's souls
About Jesus, according to you?

****

"You can be somebody,"
Is what my Momma would often say
And I have been using those words
In my life to keep me strong
When I think about a lowly Carpenter
Whose birthplace, the people said was all wrong.

****

Wishing Upon a Star

I remember a time of innocence in the springtime of my life when life was so carefree. Basically, all we had to do was eat, sleep, and play. Well, during these winter days of my life, I look back upon some of the whimsical things we did as kids.

I remember when the mosquitos started their hunting and singing as dusk was approaching, even we children stopped playing long enough to watch the appearing of the first star of the night. Often, we would gaze in wonder at that star and recite this little childhood verse:

Starlight
Star bright
First star I see tonight
I wish I may
I wish I might
Have this wish I wish tonight.

Then we would fall out laughing at being the first one to finish saying it, and our last round of playing would begin for the night. We knew it would not be long before bedtime was called.

Aa–h

The simple joys of those days so long ago
That went so fast, though at the time
Their passing seemed so slow.
The wishing upon a star was just a childhood delight
But Benevolence was listening
On many of those childhood nights
To our childhood prayers prayed in earnest
For help in our coming life plights.
Little did we know
That we would one day look back
Upon those childhood prayers of long ago
And follow them down through the years
To realize that the Benevolence that carried us from back then
To the season that we now live in
Was/is God in His lovingkindness and amazing grace
Showered upon us as a part of the human race.
As I continue my trek through the wintertime of my life,
I realize that bedtime may be called at any given moment
But I can tell you this, I never envisioned
That I would author as many books as I have and
That when I spoke, people would take a moment or so to listen.
I never knew what heights I would be allowed to gain
And I do not know how much elevation for me remains
But I can tell you this, "No amount of fortune
And no amount of fame
Can make me forget those simple childhood days
When only Jesus knew my name
I was little Alma, then and today, though wiser
I pretty much remain the same.
The world may see me as teacher, author,
or speaker extraordinaire
But I see little Alma, who the Lord lifted(s) into the air.

To think… when we, as children, scattered and played on the run
That out of our group, even then, Benevolent Eyes were
Watching me and saying, "She will be the one…"

****

I was often told as I grew up, "Remember what I told you," as I am sure some of you were, too. Those words have served me well. As a matter of fact, they have been serving me my entire life, when I heeded them. Yes, when I look back on the yesterdays of my life, whether near or far, I can see how the things my Momma told me have served me well.

I can see the time I left home and thought, "I am grown now, and nobody can tell me what to do anymore. I am an adult." Ha, ha, ha, that is laughable right now because I can also remember some of the skirmishes and missteps I had or made because I did not listen or remember what my Momma had told me. I remember some of the skinned knees I got, though.

To this day, I read my Bible as I was taught to do when I was just a child. I pray first for an understanding of what I read.
I was reading my Bible yesterday and I came upon the Scripture that will continue to carry me through my trials, burdens, grief, happy times, etc. as I make my way on through life.

"God's favor is for a lifetime."
(Psalms 30:5–6)

I did not remember, as happens to all of us on occasion, this particular Scripture, per se.

But I laid my last sibling to rest yesterday. Yet, I know I do not walk alone for God walks beside me. After the loss of my last brother, I walked through the garden of Psalms and my soul was strengthened and my spirit was reassured and renewed. I realized once again how the words of my Momma rang true, "Remember what I told you, "God will always take care of you."

I sought God's favor early on in life and received it. And I have His word that it will continue. It just does not get any better than that, y'all. How sweet it is to walk through the garden of Psalms with Jesus as your companion, something my Momma taught me when I was just a child. Yes, yes, my mother's lessons serve me well, lessons given me when I was very young.

Making the Connection

I have heard people say, "It always amazes me how fate offers us all the tools we need, to do what we were always meant to do." NO, MA'AM! NOT FATE, BUT GOD! God gave me the wisdom to be good at writing stories, writing poetry, public speaking, encouraging others, etc. and this is something I have used throughout each aspect of my life as a Christian whether as a teacher, minister's wife, mother, writer, etc.

Look back through your life for a bit and see if you don't find that to be true for you as well. Um hum–m, see I told you. But don't let your perusing stop there. What is it that you have always loved to do and were good at? Wouldn't it be wonderful if you had a job, since you work anyway, a job that allowed you to do just that? And better yet, you could incorporate your love and zeal for the Lord into your work. I did as a teacher of thirty years, a housing coordinator of ten years, a minister's wife of forty–two years and now as a writer.

I hope this Practical #3, though long, has blessed you and I further hope that you will try to think about the things you enjoy and figure out ways you can do them to the glory of God and that it works well for you as you develop your ministry (things that you do to and for the glory of God.)

I don't have adequate words to express
To you, the way that I feel that I have been blessed
You see, it means so much when you receive
A blessing whose magnitude shows God's touch.
So, this last verse is to You, Lord
I can't tell you how much I love You
But I will continue to try to show
The glory that You have allowed in me
For the world to get to know
For it is not by me that these words have been coined
But by You, masterful Father, You, Who, are Number One!
(excerpt from **Chopping My Row**, *"Blessing in and After the Storm," p. 47.)*

Just as I was equipped as a child for ***my "now,"*** I realize that my now is equipping me for my future. In other words, each stage of my life gets me ready for the next phase. This is an ongoing process as long as we inhabit the land of the living. And another thing, allow me to toss this out to you, when you are going through a tough process, it's possible you are being molded for your future work.

Practical #4: *Be Kind*

I was reading my ***Power for Today*** devotional book this morning and it was talking about the week preceding Jesus' death. The article went on to talk about how Jesus went from being adored to being degraded. You might need to read the 12th chapter of the book of John and see what I mean. *(Thank you, Danny Mize, for a great and thought–provoking article.)*

When I took the time to read the 12th chapter of John, I thought about how much the Lord loved us then and now. He suffered so much for us and all He asks in return is that we serve God and be kind to one another. He certainly gave us a fine example of being kind.

In our society today, we are so caught up with doing our own thing that sometimes we forget the simple act of saying hello. If that is all I can do for Him then I can, at least, do it well. My Momma always taught me to say, "Hello." She said that was being kind and respectful.

That is what she told me and that is what I do, but I will tell you something most of you probably already know. If you start with being kind and saying hello to your fellowman, so many things will leap out at you. Why? Because being kind covers so many different things.

Let me tell you how my being kind impacted my life.
As usual, when I want to make an application of a particular point, I ask you to walk with me as I stroll back down memory lane for examples. This topic is no different.

From as far back as I can remember, my Momma always told me to be respectful and kind to elderly people. In my child's mind, being kind and polite to them meant that Jesus would bless you because He was happy with the way you were treating His special people. Then too, I reasoned within myself that the elderly were special to Him because He had allowed them to live a good long time (Ephesians 6:3, 1 Timothy 5:1, Isaiah 46:4, 1 Peter 3:10).

I can still hear some of the elderly ladies I used to go to the store for, or sweep for, or hold the door for, or carry groceries in for, or say hello to, etc. exclaiming over how helpful or well-mannered or respectful I was.

"Little girl, you will go far! You are so kind and respectful. You watch what I say, you will go far!"

Of course, I thanked them and skipped home with a smile and told my Momma what they had said when she got home from work. But I do remember reasoning within myself that I was not going to mess with His people *(the elderly)* and have Him get mad at me.

Read Galatians 6:7 and Ephesians 6:8.

Both these verses say pretty much the same thing. If you want kindness done to you then dish out kindness to others. I remember, as a child, how special I felt when someone would do something kind to me or for me unexpectedly. I felt it was God helping me because I tried to do the right thing.

I set out to do the right thing and apparently, I succeeded because I have been blessed abundantly on my life's journey. I set out to please the Lord and He has blessed me for it. Just take a look at some of the ways He has blessed me. Besides becoming a wife and mother, He let me:

- Become a college graduate
- Become a highly acclaimed teacher

- Become a public speaker
- Become an author
- Become a poet
- Enjoy cooking
- Enjoy singing
- Enjoy crocheting and so forth.

Now I did not mention those things to brag on myself by saying I do them well. I have been allowed to be successful in the things mentioned above, but it is not me that does it. It is the glory of God shining through me. Let me explain.

When I look out at this earth that we inhabit, I see the green trees and the green grass He has carpeted it with for my little feet to walk upon. As long as the grass and trees are **still growing green** from season to season, I know God is still in control. A great reminder that "By God's Grace," or *DEI Sub Numine Viget* (Under God's Spirit I Flourish) and at the same time giving praise to my God. Yes, I do like Jeremiah 9:24 says and I brag on Him. (***Chopping My Row***, page 21)

In Book 2, ***Lift Up Your Voice***, I will tie up the results of my being kind in life in a neat package and leave you inspired to do more for God.

Practical #5: *I'm Special*

Momma told me God listened to my prayers because I was special. She told me that all people (yep, you, too) who are His children are special to Him. Then she showed me that verse in the Bible where Jesus said, "Suffer the little children to come unto me, forbid them not." I didn't tell Momma but that made me feel extra special because I was His child twice because I was a child in age and spiritually as well. *(That is something quite useful for a child to be told in this world when they are bombarded with so much – to belong to Jesus twice over. Wow!)*

You know I called you special because Jesus died for you, but that is not all. Did you know He sends forth ministering spirits to aid us? But there is still more. Here is something you may or may not have known. Jesus prayed for us before we were born! I know that is mind-boggling, isn't it? (Hebrews 1:14)

You are probably thinking, "How do you know that? And if you are going to say it is in the Bible, show me where it is written." Okay, okay, hold on, I had planned to do just that. In the book of John, chapter 17, verse 20 we read these words:

> "Neither pray I for these alone, but for them also which shall believe on me through their word..." (KJV).

If you have given your life over to Him and believe the words written about Him in the Bible, then Jesus was talking about you! These words were prayed before Jesus was ever crucified. He knew His kingdom would be established and grow. This prayer says to me that He was preparing for us way back then. You see, I told you that you were special. Uh–hum–m. I hope the info in the preceding sentence brightens your day if you were having a downer day. It certainly brightened my day when I first discovered that Scripture, and I was not even having a bad day at the time! It just made the stars in my eyes twinkle a bit more, that's all!

Don't forget that we are told more than once in the Bible that Jesus intercedes for us as He sits on the right hand of God. (Acts 7:55–56; Romans 8:34; Colossians 3:1; Hebrews 1:3; Hebrews

7:25; Hebrews 10:12; 1 Peter 3:22)

Always bear in mind that He was mindful of us before we were born and is ever mindful of us now. That, my friend, wraps me in a cocoon of assurance when life is too much. What do I do? I tell myself, "He sees, He knows, and He cares."

As we continue with our lessons in this section of our book, I want to take the time as an author and as a child of God to say I hope these series of lessons are giving you things to ponder on, as well as brightening your day.

Practical #6. *Jesus Knows Where I Am at All Times*

This means I need to trust in the Lord at all times. He knows where am going before I get there and you, too. And He will guide us.

When trouble comes, hold on and learn whatever lesson you can from it. It will pass. Everything happens for a reason and God knows what it is, indeed.

Poetry Offerings for Lesson 1

People use words in many different ways to convey all sorts of thoughts and ideas. But there have never been adequate words enough to express the heartfelt joy and thankfulness to the Creator for His tender love and care…

No, been looking a lifetime and do not find
In the vernacular, adequate enough words there
Though mankind often spends much time in prayer.
Some days, like some of you, just have to try to tell Him
What His love and ownership mean to me, especially
When I have had several moments of epiphany.
So, I tell Him "*from the tallest mountain in my world*"
As I shout to the world about the pleasure
That I have in my soul in boundless measure
To be considered His child and His treasure!

****

I tried, y'all, but I don't have enough words … To do so is a task beyond the limits of this and any other clay vessel.

I spent the better part of
My life serving people–
Fifteen years in Special Education
Fifteen years in the regular classroom
Trying to educate the youth of our nation.
Beginning with the lessons in the book
And ending with showing them all that they could bloom
As an aromatic flower in this
Garden in which we all have been planted

By becoming successful in all they undertook.
Coupled with working as a teacher
I worked forty–two years as a helpmeet
To my husband who is a preacher
No matter what congregation we went to
We tried to teach love so that the glory
Of God always came shining through.
Now, I am working fulltime on my writing
Trying to tell the world that serving
My God is not boring, but exciting.
I have built a legacy and am
Writing a good bit of it down
Allowing you to read my story and hear the voice
Of my penned words that are meant to be inspiring and sound
So that you can be taught by "Mrs. Alma," or "Sister Alma,"
Even after I am planted in the ground.

****

Trust God
When I was just a child
I learned about God's care for me
I remember thinking that God could do anything
That there was no such thing as impossibility
If He wanted a thing to be.
That belief has carried me over many a mile
And has often been the reason that I
Could endure hardship with a smile.
The years taught me the lesson of how not to worry
Because I learned what it means to serve a God, Who
Specializes in taking impossible things and proving that
There is no such thing as an impossibility when it
Comes to His love for you.

Falling Leaves
Another season is preparing to enter in
And as God allows this old world on its axis
To continue to spin
There have been some changes in some lives
That has left a hole that will never be filled again
Because one of the pieces of the puzzle is missing.
So, I speak from the lesson that time has taught me
I learned that the tears would dry and the pain would leave
And I would manage to go on, though a different person
Because I learned to grieve
Because one of the pieces of the puzzle is missing.
But through it all, the Lord brought me
And He took away my heartache
And my loneliness relieved
And left in its place a thing I truly believe
"I will get to see my loved one again
And the reunion will be just great
Because the hole will be filled and that special
Piece of the puzzle will no longer be missing
Because when I call her name, I no longer have to say, "Of late."

****

Seasons come and seasons go
And one of these seasons will see us
Grace the other side, you know
And that is okay because it is to be expected
So, let's all do a good job and do our best
As we do God's will and continue chopping our row.

****

I told Him as a child that He meant more to me than anybody in this world. I told Him I wanted to work for Him, and He has allowed me to be a bearer of joy and encouragement and I thank Him.

Get Yourself Up

Discussion Questions

1. What lesson are we as *framers of the church of tomorrow* to get from the phrase, ***"thinking little thing" even way back then?*** Tie the name of Lesson 1 in with your answer.

_____

_____

_____

_____

2. What is meant by the phrase, "***Take Jesus with you everywhere you go***?"

_____

_____

_____

_____

3. Give a Scripture that tells how the Lord feels about the elderly.

_____

_____

_____

_____

4. What do Galatians 6:7 and Ephesians 6:8 tell us?

_____

_____

_____

_____

5. As children of God, how are we special? Give a Scripture.

1 Jn 2:3 _____

_____

_____

What Do You Think?

Does God place things on children's minds today to get the attention of adults?

_____
_____
_____
_____

For Further Reading
Psalm 145:4–8

Lesson 2:

Has God Ever Really Answered Your Prayer?

Scripture: 2 Chronicles 7:14; Philippians 4:6–7; Hebrew 4:16; 1 Thessalonians 5:17

Aim: TO BE MINDFUL OF THE VALUABLE GIFT that we have in prayer.

Song: Praying Time; Jesus Is a Way Maker

"Ah–h, prayer – how important is it? Does it even work? Why bother with it?"

It goes without saying that the lessons in this book go hand in hand with prayer. These are all questions that have been asked with regards to prayer at various times in people's lives. I do hope that when we finish, those of you who believe in prayer will be buoyed up further in that belief and those of you who do not believe in it much or perhaps not at all, will be willing to give it a try and be able to say, "I prayed about it, so I am not going to worry anymore about it." (***Chopping my Row***, p. 101)

Why am I taking a whole lesson talking about prayer? Simple, it takes a whole lot of prayer to make it in this Christian life. If people are discouraged, and I write a few words to encourage them, then I am doing what the Lord has commanded me to do in Matthew 5:16 and Isaiah 50:4.

Let me tell you some of my story and what I know about God's lovingkindness to His children. I am going to tell you just a little bit about my journey through prayer and why I have such a deep abiding love for God and such an active prayer life.

Case in Point *(cont. from Lesson 1)*

Momma?

I remember crying because I wanted my Momma. And crying and crying and crying, until daddy took us to find our Momma. (Actually, it was only three days, but to my little child's brain, it was forever.) I learned later that the dirt road I remembered running across was in a little town in Mississippi called Lake Como. My Momma had run away to Memphis to her sister's house.

Daddy dropped us off to Momma at her sister's house and we were so glad to see her. Daddy talked to Momma for a while then he left. I wanted to know where he was going, and he said he would come back the next day and talk to Momma.

Well, it was two days before he came back and by then, the crybaby in me was missing her daddy something fierce. Nobody treated me special like my daddy did, so I got in a corner by myself and cried myself to sleep. I knew my daddy would be there when I woke because he always came when I cried. And he did!

Momma and daddy went back together, but this time in Memphis. Things did not work out, though. Momma finally left daddy after so many missed paychecks, women, and crying children. (She said we cried because we were hungry and that she had to use Vaseline and the last of the meal in the house to cook cornbread and feed us because there was no other food in the house. For her, that was the last straw.)

I do remember daddy coming around a couple of times and begging Momma to take him back, saying he would stop the drinking and women chasing. She gave him an emphatic, "No!" And that was the last time I saw my daddy.

"That's Just the Way It Is"

I heard those words for the first time in my life when my Momma told me with tears that my Daddy was not coming back. She said he was not going to live with us anymore. My daddy left.

After about a week to ten days, my brother started the bullying. I received a good sock in the nose, and I cried, "I'm gonna tell Dahdoo!" To which my brother replied, "You cain't tell him anything 'cause he ain't here and ain't never coming back!" Then he took my candy cane and ate it all up. I had a plan. I knew what I would do. I would cry. I knew if I cried my daddy would come. He always did. And when he came, he was gonna whip my brother for socking me in my nose and eating my candy cane, too! Yeah, right! I cried until my nose ran (and I didn't wipe it either); I cried until I had a headache, but my daddy still didn't come. I cried until I went to sleep, but when I awoke with eyes practically swollen shut, my daddy still was not there.
He never came back.

For the next two years of my life, I stopped at every AAMCO service station I saw and asked if they had a man working there named Johnny B. Carr. I was going to find my daddy! And you know what else? I carried around inside of me the thought that no matter how people treated me, I **WAS** special to my daddy! And he was going to come back to see about me, too! And I would show all the ones who laughed at me and pointed at me and sang the "You ain't got no daddy" song.

****

Momma told me years later that she used to have to go to his job to get his paycheck so he would not spend it on wine, women, and gambling. She told me the last time she had gone to his job, she ran up on his girlfriend, who was pregnant with his baby and was there to get his check, too! Momma got the check that time, but then he started taking off early to avoid giving Momma the check, or not coming in on Friday at all, which was his usual payday. As I told you earlier, the Vaseline bread was the last straw for Momma.

Favor Anyway

Though I did not have my daddy anymore it seemed like I led a charmed life. God let me find favor in the eyes of my first, second, third, and fourth grades teachers. *(If you remember the sticking a pin in the socket incident mentioned in **Chopping My Row**, well that incident happened during these years.)* At any rate, the other kids in my class referred to me as, "the teacher's pet." The word soon got around that they had better not bother me because I was the *teacher's pet*. So, I lived a somewhat sheltered life for my first nine years.

****

My mother had introduced me to Jesus by third grade, so He took the idolized place of my Daddy in my life. And unlike my daddy,

He would not leave me. I had me a new and powerful Friend! I was skipping happy!

So Many a Cloud of Witnesses

There are certain folk you can be around, and you will hear them talk about the Great God we serve and the mighty benefits of praying to Him. Too, there are certain Biblical characters that come to mind when prayer is mentioned. The Bible is full of people who kept their belief in God during hard times and showed that belief by demonstrating a prayerful life and by talking about GOD. You may have friends who laugh and joke with you and have fun, but when things get serious, and trouble comes, they turn to God in prayer and are not ashamed to let you know it.

All these people would not be touting the benefits of prayer if it did not work. This prayer thing has been passed down from generation to generation! There must be something to it. David was a man after God's own heart, and he was a strong believer in prayer. Daniel was willing to brave the lion's den because of prayer.

Y'all Were Right

Life has a way of cementing lessons in us that our parents tried so hard to instill. It has a way of making you reach back to those old lessons you got tired of hearing your parents repeat. It has a way of sending you to your parents in humble submission and saying, "Y'all were right, Mom, Dad. I just wanted to say that to you."

When we got that first prayer answered to that problem we thought would break us, we were hooked. We realized what the old folks and the saints from the Bible had been going on and on about. We had a gold mine, so to speak! Yes, folks, we were hooked on prayer. You can read about this in more detail in **Chopping My Row**, pp. 102–108.

And You Know What?

Yes, you find yourself going back again and again to the very ones you thought were old–timey and didn't know anything but the way things were done back in the day. Yes, you lose some of that cocksureness and eat a bit of humble pie. How do I know? Been there; done that! *(But as a sidenote, I have found that when you eat humble pie, you grow in grace and knowledge in the process. So take consolation in that.)*

I, who asked the Lord when I was a little girl to allow me to be somebody one day, am a strong believer in prayer. I'll mention in this lesson some of the things I went through as a child that make me know prayer works. I had heard my mother and some of the older folks talk about prayer, but oh, now! I have my own story to tell.

Why do we keep saying prayer changes things? We keep saying it because it works, and we know what life can do to a child of God if he/she is not strong! We keep saying it works because we know how we were at our ropes end and how the words of some older saint or some Bible character gave us hope enough to try prayer.

And I want to say again, "Hats off to the old timers. Y'all were right!"

If you are wondering why I keep thanking the older generation about the living examples that they showed and talked about regarding prayer, it is to try to imbed the thought of praying in your mind so that when you get in a quiet place by yourself, you will give it a try if you are not already an avid prayer. Then, too there are those who may have hit a snag in their life regarding prayer and have started to think that praying really does no good when the *chips are down*. Hogwash! Nothing is further from the truth. That is just discouragement rearing its ugly head and don't you know that is one of the biggest weapons the adversary has in his bag of tools and tricks to use against Christians?

****

By the end of this lesson, it is my aim that you be a praying person if you are not, and a stronger praying person if you already are. It is my aim that your trust and love for the Lord will have grown to the extent that you would stand on top of the tallest mountain in the world and proclaim His love for mankind and your love for Him!

"Why Do So Many Say It Is So, If It Ain't So?"
Learning to Trust Him
You just have to learn to trust Him
Even when trusting Him is hardest to do
You have to show Him your faith, though weak
Is still in Him by virtue of the great cloud
Of witnesses in the Holy Writ and by virtue
Of living witnesses that you have gotten the chance to talk to
Who continue to tell and pass down their story
About the magnificent Father that we all have in Glory.

Listening to the words of the witnesses and the fervor they display when talking about the benefits of prayer will bless your soul and just might make you want to try it if you are not already an avid prayer.

If you look around you with prayerful eyes, you will see, evidence of prayers being answered concerning the great and concerning the small. Do you remember when there were wildfires burning in several states, and when there were several hurricanes heralding toward the United States at a fierce pace? That was a time of collective praying, wasn't it? Sure, it was. That was a time when everybody who wore the name Christian remembered 2 Chronicles 7:14, KJV and acted upon it. Nobody had to tell us to begin our day with prayer or to remind us to pray. We woke up thinking about the situation and uttered a prayer right then, often before rising, didn't we?

****

Praying Time

You have a set time for eating every day, a set time for going to work, a set time for watching television, etc. In fact, you have a set time for most things that are important to you. Then, you ought to have a set time for prayer. Begin your day with it. You will be glad you did for you will find out that HE knows how to take care of you better than you do yourself, although you have been living as you all your life. (tee hee) Not so surprising, HE knew you before you were even you, and before you even knew you were you!

I recently celebrated the day of my birth. My mother, who was a preacher's daughter, often told me I was the little girl that she had wanted so badly. Well, she was granted a baby girl who looked just like her twin! People often told us that. And now, I, the daughter of a preacher's daughter, am a preacher's wife. And the fact that I am an inspirational author and poet seems to fit right into that picture, don't you think? My Momma's prayers were answered in that she got the little girl she always wanted.

But What Do You Do When the Answer Is "No"?

Nobody likes to be told "no." You don't, and neither do I. But I learned to live with God's "no" early on in life. Remember when you were still a child and you wanted to do something very badly, and your parents said, "no"? Remember how you acted?

Remember how relieved you felt when something unfavorable came to light, and you were so thankful your parents had not allowed you to go to a certain event or participate in such–and–such? If you think about it, I imagine there were several times in your life that your parent's intuition had proven to be right when it came to something you wanted to do. In the latter part of your teenage years, you probably had become resigned when you asked to go someplace or to do something, and they said "no" to such an extent that you did not throw a fit as rapidly as you used to. (I know you probably did like most of us did back then and thought you would be glad to go to college or get your own place because nobody could tell you what to do then.) But all in all, you had learned to trust your parents as if they had some inner radar for sticky situations where you were concerned.

We have learned to trust our parents, but not God? Well, yes, those are some strident words, but I believe they hold some merit, for some of us, anyway. Here is why I said what I did. When we pray for something, and it does not happen, we have been given one of three answers, which are, "Yes, no or wait a while." How long is a while? It might be soon or not so soon. It means we have to live, work, and carry on with our daily lives. If a thing is meant to happen, it will. If it is not God's will, then it will never happen, and we must learn to live with that. Look at things like this:

If it is meant to be, it will be
And if it is not meant to be
We just have to take it personally
And think, "God said no because
He knows what is best for me."

****

And remember, our parents, in their limited vision, told us, "No," and we still respect them today. How much more does God, Who sees the total picture big and small, deserve our obeisance and subjection?

So, if you did not get an affirmative answer to your prayer, you cannot justify yourself by being angry because you, the thing created, cannot chastise the Creator, the Master Planner. (Job 38, and Philippians 1:6) If He did not answer your prayer in the affirmative, trust Him and keep stepping.

Case in Point

There are several things in my life that I did not get an affirmative answer to, among which are: to have my daddy come back and to bear a child. Those two things never happened, and I am okay with that. I have told myself that God saw and sees way down the road, so He made and makes the most informed decisions. And because I trust Him, I step on.

Praying Time – When Anger Erupts

Pray on a Personal Level – A couple of months back was a very trying time for me for several reasons. I won't go into the particulars of the situation at this time, but this was one of those times that shook me like a mongrel dog does a helpless chick. It shook me so that I had to try hard to focus my mind, body, and soul on God in prayer! It shook me so that I wanted to go back to my young spitfire days and say these words, "Uh–huh, I'm gonna teach you what you forgot to learn on your mother's knee!" It shook me so that I wanted to pinch myself to see if I was dreaming because it could not be real, though it was. It shook me so that I wanted to yell, "Oh no you don't! Somebody has lost their ever-loving mind!"

But ...

I remembered Who I was living for and had been living for most of my life and called on Him. When I say I called, folks, I sho' nuff called! My mind, body, and soul called on Him. If my sweat pores and hair follicles could, they called on Him, too. I was that distressed, y'all. But not anymore. "What a difference prayer and a day makes!" I girded up my loins and acted as a Christian ought to act while I took appropriate actions.

There is a verse in the Bible that says, "Be angry and sin not." (Ephesians 4:26, KJV) It did not say don't get angry; it said when and if you do get angry, don't let that anger cause you to sin. What I got hit with would cause most of you as mothers, whether Christian or not, to grind your teeth and want to jump into action. But I did not jump into action the way I initially wanted to. Instead, I went into warrior prayer mode, right then and right there! And I prayed the whole time I was talking on the phone, the whole time I was getting ready for my meeting, the whole time I was driving to the meeting, the whole time I was walking across the parking lot to the meeting place and in the meeting itself. As a result of my prayers, I was able to conduct myself in an appropriate Christian manner while making my extreme concerns known. At the end of the meeting, which stayed businesslike, but turned somewhat cordial, I brought my baby home.

I had often heard my Momma talk about praying her anger away and I just did not get it. But oh, now I do. And so begins another chapter in my life with my daughter back at home from the group home. Today, a tenuous peace reigns in my world. I take each moment as it comes as I have for over forty years.

Well, I can tell you one thing, the last forty years have not been dull, and I who always asked for patience, almost have the patience of Job, well, maybe not quite, but I'm working on it. (smile)

As I have said earlier, you should have a set time to pray. And I advise people, "Begin your day with prayer because when you do, God is already in attendance with you in whatever your day brings your way. And you will be able to prayerfully to continue to walk your life path."

Pray on a National Level – Recently, there have been some events in the news that have rocked us in our complacent little world. We have all been made to go back to the old-time way when praying was done more than once a day and more than just for our families. Whether we realize it or not, our families can thrive only as well as our nation thrives, thus our world. Have you prayed for our nation and our world lately? Have you prayed for our leaders and the leaders of this world, lately? It's time.

Praying Time for All

Don't listen to the news and shake your head
And don't hide your head in the sand
Do what we have been taught that generations
Have done through the ages and pray
God's blessings all over the world's lands.
History has taught us that President Roosevelt
Called for a National Day of Prayer and
Asked Americans everywhere
To stop what they were doing at a certain
Hour to pray and Heaven was bombarded
With many prayers that day
Because the people had used their
Collective prayer voices in a powerful way.
"If my people who are called by my name
Will humble themselves, I will hear from Heaven…"
And y'all, remember that we pray to the God of Biblical fame.
Worried about your family and what is going to come to pass?
No need, just do what generations before us have done
And bow your knees, everyone
Because many a prayer was prayed by loved ones long gone
And now, it is up to us to strengthen that decaying foundation
That will shore up our families and carry them on.
Let "Praying Time" be the battle call of the day
And watch hatred abscond and love seep in to stay
While problems that seemed insurmountable fade away.

I can just imagine what would have happened if I had not invited
Jesus to help me when my child was accosted the way that she
was in the trying situation that I mentioned previously! Whew!
Thank God for His amazing and saving grace.

What Would Happen

Can you imagine what would happen if all of us were to allow our prayerful love to meet at God's throne at a certain time on a given day? Uhm, hmm–m and to even have the little ones involved in the silent praying. God does hear children, you know. *(And besides, that would be a good practice for the children in the art of learning reverence in prayer.)*

Biblical history, written secular history, and oral history have all told us of the benefits of prayer. And I have told you several times that things do happen when people collectively pray. I mean think about it. **Really think about it.** Why do you think so many rulers and dictators down through time did not want praying going on? Hmm–m? Exactly, because it works!

Soldier of the School of Prayer

Just a note of remembrance from an old soldier of the school of prayer. Oftentimes we are bombarded with so much in life that we have to be reminded to get up off of the stool of worry and do nothing and go down on our knees in prayer.

The Bible says "Whatsoever things were written before time were written for our learning." (Romans 15:4) So, when you have times like the ones mentioned in the first paragraph, in your life, go back to the Bible and see the value of prayer.

Paul and Silas were imprisoned for doing the Lord's work and prayer brought them out. Learn from that. (Acts 16:25–34, KJV) Peter was imprisoned for doing the Lord's work and prayer brought him out. Learn from that. (Acts 12:1–17)
If you have a prayerful grandmother, mother, aunt, cousin, or a

church member you admire, go to them and ask them to tell you about a couple of times that they were between a rock and a hard place and how the Lord God brought them out. Learn from that!

As you learn, you and your faith will grow stronger
Burdensome problems will worry you no longer
And you will step as you did in your carefree days
When you and your faith were so much younger.

****

As I have discussed in my book, ***Chopping My Row***, you will learn to give your problems to Him and suddenly or gradually realize that since you have become committed to a life of prayer, that, though the problems are the same, you aren't. (***Chopping My Row***, p. 95, 111) You will realize you now have sweet peace that defies reason.

And how did you get such sweet relief? By going to the Lord God in prayer, that's how! That relief comes from knowing the Lord will make a way somehow.

And that, folks, is how Sister Alma keeps on smiling.

I am blessed in my doings because I have learned to always take it to Jesus.

I cannot say this too many times – always begin your day with prayer. Always! You see, you don't know if a given day is the day you will meet old trouble, but you do know that if you begin your day with prayer, God will be by your side and will walk with you through whatever trouble you may encounter. Why, because you gave Him an invitation at the beginning of your day.

Be blessed with insight, as you ponder these thoughts.

And if you should find yourself in a situation where you rushed into your day and did not get your praying time in, don't fret.

You don't have to be on your knees to pray to God. You can pray wherever you are and in whatever situation you are in. If you find yourself on the bottom of the ocean, you can pray from there.

How do I know? Jonah did, didn't he? Uh hum–m.

Equipped

I want you to be equipped enough so that you are able to do what I do when life throws me several curved balls, and I feel overwhelmed. I want you to do like I do and remember to reach back into your arsenal of faith and use your tool of prayer that hopefully you will develop or further develop. I want you to know just like I know that God sees, knows, and cares about you just like a mother does with her newborn child.

You see, when I go to Him in prayer, He never turns me away, even when I have not done all that I should have. All I have to say is, "Father, please forgive and help me."

Let me tell you something. I never go anyplace nor try any new venture without the Lord. That is why I have practically made a song out of **BYDWP**. Let me put it in different phraseology. When you go into the day without prayer, that is like a soldier going into battle with nothing but goodwill. Can you imagine David going up against Goliath without the Lord, armed with only goodwill?! Ha Ha, I think not!

Get Yourself Up

Just as Momma had me to build my life around prayer and reading my Bible, my Gran Gran underscored that practice for me by stressing the same things. I am doing the same for you. Why? I am doing so because just like the two godly women mentioned in the preceding sentence stressed those practices for me because they loved me and knew that one day, maybe after they were gone, life would have a go at me, I want to similarly equip you. And as far as life having a go at me, oh my word, were they right!

You see, this praying person has known poverty, faced traps set by enemies, been the victim of racism and jealousy, etc. But when confronted with the things mentioned above, I remembered what my Momma taught me and utilized that teaching by praying about any problem I had. You are reading the book of a person who has been the recipient of answers to prayers prayed, and to cite a few:

- Prayed my way out of poverty
- Prayed my way past racism
- Prayed my way over traps
- Prayed my way past the limits that another's jealousy would have set
- Requested that the saints help me by praying for me because I remembered what the Bible said about praying for one another. (Prayers of the righteous availeth much, James 5:16, KJV)

Lastly

As I have said many times before, "For peace that surpasseth all understanding," (Philippians 4:7, KJV) get your praying time in.

I know He is with me wherever I go because He has told me so. He has allowed me to get close to Him and allowed me to stay close to Him. That is why I don't worry much about given situations. I have learned to give it over to God and let Him handle it. I know He loves me and I know His shoulders are broader than mine. I further know that when I whimper, He knows. Know that when life brings me to tears, He knows; when I laugh, He knows; when I get exasperated, He knows, etc. He sees and knows all about me and continues to sustain me and bring me unsurpassable peace in all situations. That's the God I serve. That is why I received a homespun "Pollyanna Award" from the writers' group I am a part of.

That is why you might hear me singing the words:

"Get your time in–n–n, it's praying time. Get your time i–i–n–n, it's praying time. Oh hallelujah! It's praying time."

Pray
Get your prayer in this morning or today
Always know that it is important
To make the time to pray
When you get too busy for prayer
You, my friend, have too many things
Crammed into your day.

Case in Point

I want to give you as much encouragement as I can regarding prayer. Here is another *case in point* for you.

You have seen those old mafia movies where the mafia boss' word is a law unto itself. No one willingly crosses a mafia boss, right?

So, in our scenario today let's say that a man is at the end of his rope and is close to giving up. His wife and two-month-old baby will be evicted from their apartment in three hours. There is a shelter they can go to, but not as a family. Joey B. is a family man and vowed when he married his Stella to always provide for her. There are no close family members left. They are on their own. Then a friend from his childhood says to him, "Joey B, I know this guy that might be able to help you. I mean, what you got to lose, huh?"

At the Mafia Boss' Office

Yep, you guessed it. Joey B. goes to see this mafia boss, and the mafia boss says, "What's the problem, Joey B? I knew your old man from back in the day. He was a square guy who kept his nose clean." Joey B. tells the mafia boss his problem, and the mafia boss says, "No problem, Joey B. I will take care of it."

Because the mafia boss was a man of his word, the eviction never happened, and Joey B. got a regular job as maintenance supervisor at a new factory and moved from the basement to a bigger apartment so there was a bedroom for the baby.
Joey B. was fortunate that his father had been such a square guy that the mafia boss liked, huh? He knew someone who was powerful!

POWER

Well, WHO do you think is more powerful, JEHOVAH GOD or some mafia boss? Exactly! That is my point! You have access to the most powerful POTENTATE that has ever been or ever will be. And HE loves you.

Read Hebrews 4:16.

In that Scripture, the Lord says to you, (and I am paraphrasing,) "Do you, oh child of MINE, have a problem? Tell me about it. You can approach MY throne at any time, and I will hear your request and take care of you. But you have to be faithful to ME, and you have to ask. I know how to take care of you because I created you. Do you hear ME? You are MINE, and I love you more than you know. Always remember that. Now, what's your problem?"

(I did take poetic license with this passage, but the meaning is clear. You have a FATHER, WHO sits on the throne of Heaven and all HIS resources are available for supplying your needs. We need to recognize Who He is because, folks, it just does not get any better than that!)

So, if there ever comes a time when life has your back against the wall, you just keep praying and believing.

God will work things out for you if you keep your faith intact, no matter what your enemies plan. No matter what state we are in, in our lives, we must never forget to pray. Remember, have a set time to pray every day. Read the poem below:

Do you do your best talking to Jesus in the
Wee hours of the morning before the break of day
Me too, don't know what it is about that time
But it is then that I can articulate best what I want to say.
It is easy for me to approach His
Throne at that early hour
So, that I can bask in His love and in
His infinite sense of power.
—excerpt from ***Chopping My Row***

****

No matter what we are going through
Begin your day with prayer and peace of mind
Is what you will find.

****

Hebrew 4:16 – Know this Scripture and put it into practice. I can never get enough of the knowledge and the experience of prayer because the more I learn, the more I yearn.

Are You a Worrier or a Pray-er?
I told you before that I have always been a deep thinker and that I spent 30 years as a teacher. Yes, if you guessed that I had my

students thinking deeply you are correct. I did indeed teach my students to become deep thinkers, for which, I still get "Thank You's" to this day. And you know folks, all I was doing, was performing my job by teaching my kids to want to learn by teaching them to love to learn! You did not hear me, so I am going to say it one more time. I taught my children to want to learn by teaching them to love to learn.

And I have been trying to do the same thing for you. Say what! Yes, you heard me correctly. Teaching you to want to pray by teaching you to love to pray. Not for all of you because some of you are way ahead of me and I applaud you. But for the sake of the others, stay with me as I break it down to them, okay?

Driving the Point Home

How many of you have something on your mind worrying you? Well, listen to this. There are one or two reasons why you worry, whether you realize it or not.

You don't pray **OR** You don't trust God.

There are no two ways about it. If you trust Him, you will pray and not worry about your problem anymore. But you have to know Him in order to trust Him and, too, you have to have a history with Him. Sometimes as we are struggling to live this life down here, situations can get to be too much for us, and we feel like we cannot do it any longer. News flash! Worrying about it will not make it go away but praying about it *sho'* will.

My advice to you is to seek to get close to HIM because when you get close to the Lord, you will find that closeness nourishes your soul, and you will find yourself snuggling up to Him more and more because to know Him is to love Him. You will find yourself receiving nourishment from your prayerful study of His word and your daily presence before His throne, for you will become a person who wants to pray because you have learned to love to pray. Here's what you do:

- Start your day off with Him. Don't wait until your life is a mess before you go seeking Him. And don't seek Him later in the day after you have gotten to work or taken care of pressing needs, etc. Don't relegate God to the fringes of your life. When you meet a cherished friend, you don't ignore them until it is convenient, do you? No, you don't, so don't do similar things to our Lord. Okay? If you will put Him first, He will be near at all times. This is what I have found to be true through the years.

- Make sure your life is free from sin. Always keep yourself in a condition that you not only can pray for yourself and others but that you do it.

- Thank Him for His lovingkindness, justice, and righteousness. Remember I told you that He delights in these things. (Jeremiah 29:11)

- Don't forget the Scripture that says the "Prayers of the righteous availeth much." (James 5:16, KJV) Use the members of the church to help you through your Johnson grass or stormy times. Though they are chopping rows of their own, they will come together to help you if you ask. You are all in the field of cultivating souls, and they are working right alongside you.

- Address the Father with thanks for previous blessings.

- Ask for the building up of your faith daily as you begin your day with prayer.

- Ask the Father for what you desire.

- Ask in belief.

- Ask in Jesus' name.

- Give your prayers power by showing love and praying for more than your family. Pray for the church leaders and the preacher, too. When was the last time you prayed for the less fortunate, the church leaders, the church as a whole and the church worldwide, world peace? (James 5:16) Remember in Luke 8, Jesus was moved with compassion because of the multitude and their need.

If you can feel the love through this book I have written for Him, good! Dear one, you feel that love because He first loved me and asked me to love you, too. And so I do. (John 13:34–35)

Let me put it another way. Can a true mother ever get too busy to answer her child's cries for help if the child is being threatened by a mongrel dog or what–have–you? Exactly! Then neither can the Lord God. All He asks is that we have faith in Him and that we show that faith and love by seeking chat time with Him (praying). He likes to hear from us. (Hebrews 4:16, KJV) What? Why, of course, He knows your name! He counted the hairs on your head, didn't he?

I am teaching you to value prayer by showing you how much He loves you. I want prayer to be your natural defense mechanism. You know I have often told you to **BYDWP**, but there are times in life when you use prayer much like air. Practically every breath is an inhaled or exhaled prayer. That is what happens during supercell storm times! Been there and done that. (sigh)

But I find that through the praying and breathing, somewhere along the road the load gets easier to bear. That is what is meant by "the storm becoming your norm." (***Chopping My Row***, p. 94)

How to Handle Answered Prayers

Don't be surprised at the blessings when you stay faithful to GOD, for HE will "work things out for your good" (Romans 8:28). Start preparing for those blessings, even if you only prepare yourself mentally. I must confess, I have been blown away by some of the blessings I received after some of my supercell storms have ended. It gives further credence to the old song that says, "You can't beat God's giving, no matter how you try." I know this song was written about the giving of time, money, etc., to the Lord and His subsequent blessings. But I am speaking of the giving He has done for mankind (His Son) and of His knowing us so well, that He can satisfy us to the very fiber of our being! How Swee–e–et to be loved by God! I just love being loved by Him and I love trying to love Him back!

Strong Tower

One of the things I always saw my mother do was kneel and pray. She taught me to kneel and pray, too. I was a little hardheaded about some things, but prayer was not one of them. When I was younger and had just gotten out on my own, I did not know how to lean on the Lord totally. But when sickness hit my mother or my children, and I had been to all the doctors, and had done all I could do, that is when I learned to lean on Him.

Strong Tower Not So Strong Anymore

You see, Momma had always been my strong tower, my go–to–person. But the strong tower was not so strong anymore. And my children, they looked to me like **I** had all the answers and like they knew I would make everything all right. I began to understand what my Momma felt when my dad chose drinking and women instead of living with us and providing for us and there we were, looking to her!

The Tables Were Turned

But I had a moment of panic because the Strong Tower was leaning on me! What was I going to do?! I learned to lean on the Solid Rock. I learned to call Him in times of plenty, health, sickness, at midnight, etc. I learned to lean on Him and realized that He never got tired of me. I learned to lean and realized that He would not ever leave me. I understood my Momma's words when she said the Lord was faithful and always would provide and would never, never leave me all alone.

When I began to despair because it seemed that everybody was leaning on me, my faith told me that if I just did like David said in Psalm 27:14, "Wait on the Lord," that everything would be all right. So, I prayed, and I waited.

So, don't be surprised one day when you are called upon to be the strong tower in the family. Just like I realized that because of my past with Him, God would handle everything, you will come to that realization, too. I knew God would handle everything because I remembered I had my share of doubts, fears, troubles, with valleys to go through and hills to climb. I remembered He brought me through it all, and He let me know that when I got too tired He was with me and that the reward in the after while would be worth it all.

More Show–N–Tell

You will receive answers to prayers. And nothing in this world lies beyond the reach of prayer unless it lies beyond the will of God. Knowing and remembering these two facts are handy tools to keep in your arsenal of faith and should help you remember to not be surprised when He does answer.

Case in Point

Realize that prayer did not go out of business in Biblical days. There is no Gone to Lunch sign on the door of God's prayer answering business.

Responses to a couple of my poems on my social media set my teeth on edge. Someone wrote on my Twitter feed that *God was not real!* This was written in response to a couple of poems I wrote about God and His goodness and His love for us. Well, you know that set my teeth on edge. But immediately following that sentiment came pity. I mean this person's life must have been some kind of messed up for a person to think that. They may have had hardships aplenty. I can only hope they find the Lord God before it is too late.

The response to the poems on my blog made me do some deep reflecting, but one incident comes to mind readily because it is forever emblazoned in my memory. Before I tell you of that incident, let me tell you how I responded to the person who made the negative comment about God. Did I ever lay down a few home truths, but all done in love, mind you. All done in love. This is what I said.

If God is not real, then:

1. How did the Bible know way before modern science did that there were channels in the sea?

2. How does a person know to call a family member just on a "gut feeling," and find out they are in an emergency situation?

3. Why do the enemies of Christians get so disturbed when Christians begin to pray? It surely could not be because they are praying to a mighty God Who is not real! Hmm–m–m? That's what I thought, you'd say.

4. Who took a penniless little nobody, put a song in her heart, joy on her lips, and wrapped her up in such optimism that people have been heard to exclaim, "Ain't nobody that happy!" Who gave her a Pollyanna disposition? Who singled her out so that the world would take note and seek her out for some of the words of wisdom that she prayed for daily as a child? Surely not God because He is not real! Really? Well, you cannot prove it by me because He lives in this once penniless nobody's soul!

5. And one last sweet note, Who gave the birds such a pretty song to sing? It was Somebody bigger than you and me. Help me say to the world:

"God is, was, and always shall be!"

I did not take the time to expound upon all the facts that ascertain God is not only real, but that He is really powerful as well.

Did I neglect to mention that He is so loving He forgives time after time? Yes, even the ones who have disavowed Him. He is just that merciful and I am glad because I, as we all are, am a sinner saved by grace.

The Incident Forever Emblazoned in My Memory

The temperature was 18° on a frigid January day down in Memphis, Tennessee. There was a little girl of about 80 pounds struggling against the cold wind on her mile and a half walk home.

Imagining that walk, you realize the child would be cold through and through. But having to go home to a house with no water, no lights, and most importantly, no heat, you know the child was a picture of cold abject misery. That child was me. But wait a minute. Yes, I was miserably cold, but I had Something on the inside of me that pushed me onward with my Momma's words ringing in my ears, "You gon be somebody one day!"

Look at This

• *DEI Sub Numine Viget* is the name of one of my books of poetry and do you know what those words mean? That is Latin for, "Under God's Spirit, She Flourishes."

• There is another saying of mine I have as a cover page for my iPad. That saying is, "God is the only reason I made it this far!"

• And in the same vein, there is a song I hum and sing every now and then with these words:

"By the grace of the Lord, I've
Come a long, long way
Oh by the grace of the Lord, I've
Come a long, long way.

When the storms of life are raging
Oh Lord, stand by me
When this old world tosses me
Like a ship out on the raging sea
Thou Who ruleth the wind and waters
Hmm–m–m, stand by me!" (public domain)

****

If I take poetic license and apply it to my life the last verse of that song would go something like this:

When the storms of Alma's life got(get) to raging
Hmm–m–m, my God stood (stands) by me
When this old world grabbed (grabs) me and tossed (tosses) me
Like a ship out on the raging sea
The God Who ruleth winds and the waters
Said (says), "Stop! Alma belongs to Me–e–e."
****

Today is a time for praise because somebody out there needs to be reminded that:

God Is
God is still
Handling His business
Of which you are chief.

If this world has a bad hold on you and is shaking you like a mongrel dog does a helpless chick so that your head flops every which way, keep your eyes and mind on God and keep sending up those prayers. He will deliver you, and as I can attest to the fact, He will provide! You see:

Back then,
- It was 18° that January day
- With no water, lights, or heat
- Brr–rr!

Oh, but now,
- January 2019 18° with a central heating system that comes on when the temperature drops a few degrees and keeps every corner of my home the same warm temperature
- Hot water when I want it for bathing and cold water when I want a refreshing drink
- Electric lights throughout my home with a light that comes on in the clothes dryer, refrigerator, and garage when you open the door
- When I need to go to the store, there is an SUV parked in the garage that I can push a button to warm it up before I get in it. And let's not forget the heated seats and steering wheel if I want them turned on. That little girl no longer has to walk 1.5 miles in the cold being buffeted by the wind.

There are so many Scriptures that talk about waiting on the Lord. Those Scriptures say that if you wait on the Lord, He will come through for you and rout your enemies in the process.

Take the Scripture I read today, Psalm 52:8–9 says:

8 But I am like a green olive tree in the house of God: I trust in the mercy of God for ever and ever.

9 I will praise thee forever, because thou hast done it: and I will wait on thy name; for it is good before thy saints.

In verses 1–7, of Psalm 52, the Lord routed my enemies, but that is not where I got my main point for today. When I look at verses 8 and 9 of Psalm 52, I see a soul much like mine. I see a soul who has been blessed and fed and watered and one who has learned to lean on and trust in God. You see that green olive tree is surrounded by abundance. That is me. I am amply provided for and have learned by my years of walking with God that He will take care of, provide for, and love me.

Come a Long Way

I cannot tell you all that the Lord has brought me through
So, say what you want to or say what you will
But this old soldier is grateful
To the God of Heaven Who carries me, still.

Thanking God for blessings and offering thanksgiving and praise for being able to live in my "one day." You see, when I was a child, I prayed continually to be able to go to college and become a teacher and to be somebody one day. That happened for me, folks. The Lord orchestrated a way for me to go to college and become a teacher. He allowed me to become such a success as a teacher that some of my former students still reach out to me on Facebook from time to time.

Case in Point

As a matter of fact, two days ago, I got a message on Facebook from a former student of mine, basically saying I had made a great impact on his life. He told me I made my class so relatable that he wished I could have been his teacher the next year and the year after that. He told me he was sure I heard that all the time. But contrary to what he thought, I do not hear that all the time, as a matter of fact, seldom.

Case in Point

That was what made me do a doubletake when I received a message from another former student of mine this morning! She said she wanted to reach out to someone she had always looked up to and that I was one of those. We had such a nice chat, and I told her how nice it was to hear from her after all these years. I went on to ask her if life had been kind to her and if she was doing all right. She told me she had not been doing well in January, but that she was doing all right, now. We chatted for quite a bit, with her catching me up on a lot of things that had happened to her over the years. We said we would keep in touch and I promised her I would pray for her, which I did, silently, as we were texting back and forth.

Case in Point

A Mini Vacation
When I awoke one morning back in the early summer, I began to look upon the day like a mini vacation. Here is how my mini vacation came about.

I had been asked to do a poem and a song on a program in Memphis later in the afternoon, so we opted to spend the entire day there, in the city of my birth. I made plans to meet an old college roommate of mine at the program, and while in the city, I stopped by to see a favorite cousin of mine, Essie, whom I had not seen in almost twenty years.

I also sold several of my books at the places we frequented.

Yep, just one day away from the usual grind and I felt like a new person. I really must say I was not prepared for people's reaction to the poem of mine, a portion of which, I had set to music when I wrote it. *(No, I do not read nor write music, but I hummed that song of mine and hit the corresponding keys on the piano, that sounded like what I sang, to my ear anyway.)* The end result was a catchy little tune that when I sang it down in Memphis, the audience grabbed hold of it. Y'all, they sang along with me and stood and clapped and clapped. The poem was "Ultimately," from pages 31 – 34, of **Chopping My Row**. I won't bother to type the whole poem for you because you can look it up in the book, but I will type the introductory verse that I added to the poem expressly for the occasion.

But here's the kicker, the thing that made my day overflow with astounding joy. When I finished my song on the program, one person asked me for my autograph. We had a good laugh about that, but I can say I had a stress–free day.

Imagine the dead of winter with no lights, water, or gas
With a charcoal bucket as the only way of heating and cooking
Imagine grass two–feet high in the front yard in the summertime
And nothing you could do about it but heave a sigh
Now imagine a loving mother's words always saying to you
'Baby, always reach for the sky.'
That was my life from about eleven years old to 18 years old
And since those years, y'all, I have traveled a winding and
mountainous road.

In the above poem, I talked about my years after turning 18, graduating high school and heading off to college. I told the audience yesterday that it was on that winding and mountainous road I became acquainted with ultimately.

When I finished that poem and my two snippets of songs, as I told you earlier, the applause was deafening and almost every heart in the place, I held for a few moments in my hand. God's grace! I had a very enjoyable day, and I thank God for providing it for me. God's grace in providing a one–day mini vacation. His providential love knows no bounds.

God has done it and my cup runs over with the need to tell my story about His lovingkindness and justice and righteousness! I can't tell it all, but I am going to tell it until I can no more. No, I won't be shushed because when a ballplayer or golfer or tennis player or some other sports player does something great, we talk about it for days on end! We figure the player did it and deserves to be talked about and praised. Well, that is my rationale for talking nonstop about Him and singing an unbroken song about His goodness.

"God has done it, and I will give Him thanks forever." It's that simple, folks, just that simple.

My "One Day"

God has answered my prayers I prayed so many years ago as a child, to "Let me be somebody, one day." He brought it to my attention two days ago and yet again, this morning. It is almost like He served it up to me on a silver platter, "Alma Carr Jones, you are somebody. You are living to see your, 'one day,' that you prayed about as a child. Enjoy, little one, enjoy."

Listen, Let Me Tell You
If you have a problem that you cannot solve
Put it in the hands of God and
Watch your problems dissolve.
Over the years, I've laid my problems at His feet
And the finesse with which He handled them
I tell you, just cannot be beat.

So, I can say to all people, both in the church and out of it, that God is faithful, and it pays to remain close to Him. I can stand and give my testimony for the Lord, and I do it with no shame. I'm proud to be a worker in God's vineyard, and I will tell it wherever I go!

My Point

Am I bragging about what I have been able to gain in my life? No Sir and No Ma'am! What I am doing is bragging about how the God I serve will provide! I am just another one of His children telling you He will provide. So, you keep praying and keep hoping as you learn to keep still, and one day after God has delivered you, you will be singing your own song and telling your own story to God's glory just like me.

Just as the verse below says, He took me from the ash heap and set me at the table with nobles, and I am able to speak from the tallest mountain in my world. And though I yell, y'all, I just can't tell it all!

From the Ash Heap to the Mountain Top
From the ash heap to the mountain top
Is where God brought me to in my life
And I will keep working for Him
Y'all, I will not, and I cannot stop
Because He deserves my glory and my praise
So my voice in gratitude to Him I raise.
He is glorious
He is victorious
Our God's love and
Works are meritorious.

*(The poem above came out in the shape of a cup! If water were in
the goblet, I suppose I could raise it in salute to our most
awesome God! Or it could be symbolic of Jesus' shed blood.
Wow, now that is an attention getter! My cup overfloweth …)*

A Few Wrap Up Tips

Hoping you learn to love to pray and that you get a Scripture
motto that feeds your soul just like my Momma and I did.

"The Lord God has given Me
The tongue of the learned,
That I should know how to speak
A word in season to him who is weary.
(Isaiah 50:4, NKJV)

As I have said before, God has people like me to tell you what He
has done for us. Why? So you will remember or learn that He is
faithful and that He will take care of you and your cares, too. If
you believe in Him, that is. God wants you to present all your
cares to Him and leave His throne with a lightheartedness that

you may not have known for quite some time. He will take care of you because He loves you; He is faithful, and He has written it in the Holy Writ to give you assurance. (Hebrews 4:16)

You see, if I tell you often enough, with enough passion and with enough conviction, you will be convinced enough to try Him yourself. All it takes is a little belief (a little faith), and He will handle the rest. And then ... it will be like an avalanche.
Folk will start to ask you how you are making it through whatever trials and or troubles you have with such lack of worry. And that is when you start to tell your story just like I have been telling mine. Yes, you will tell your story because you want to always stay in good standing with Him, so you will do the things He has asked you to do, such as:

1. Loving others the way you want Him to love you,

2. Asking for forgiveness of your sins as you forgive others,

3. Thanking Him for answered prayer,

4. Spreading the knowledge of His goodness to your brother, sister, and neighbor and giving them the tool to take their situation apart and analyze it and come up with the same puzzled and wondrous summation that you did – that though their problem may be the same as it was an hour or day before prayer, that they are different because they no longer are worrying about it! Uh oh! Another one will have been taught to pray and to learn to love it.

5. Going on about your day, doing good wherever you can with a smile, a kind deed, etc. Always be mindful

of the fact that this may be the day you might pick up a motto similar to mine, "Doing What I Can While I Can" or my Momma's, "In Thee, Oh Lord, I Put My Trust."

This portion of our lesson is a tribute to my Momma, the preacher's daughter, through her favorite Scripture, Psalm 31:1 and Psalm 71:1.

"In Thee, Oh Lord, I Put My Trust," was my Momma's favorite Scripture.

I shared the impact Psalm 71 had on me one day during a moment of meditation and prayer in *Chopping My Row*. It has since become my favorite passage of Scripture during my twilight years. But what I find ironic is that her favorite passage of Scripture turned out to be mine, now. No, I did not know where it was located in the Bible, I just know she quoted it so much, I knew it by heart. Is it too much of a coincidence that the same passage of Scripture speaks to me, too? If you don't get why I am floored to learn that the passage of Scripture that rocks me during my dark times and shields my joy, happens to be the same one that fed my Momma's soul, you just keep living; you will understand someday. But I tell you one thing, I see the hand of God in that passage and in the fact that He allowed it to become such a part of my Momma that it was ingrained in me.

You see, He knew that after she had made her departure to the other side that there would come some dark times in my life when that Scripture would bathe my soul in hope as it shepherded me to His throne. Oh my soul, what a mighty God we serve! I find that I was yet again in His training camp, even as a child and I didn't even know it!

9/12/21

C Folks

Listen to me, folks. If you do not remember much else that I have said, remember this: If you keep your hand in God's hand, He will train you for His work and bring you full circle, right back to His throne. You will venture out into the world, but you will come back to Him a little broken and maybe a little chipped and chiseled, but so much stronger in your resolve to work for Him and to stay close to Him through your God-given avenue of prayer because you realize He is where your hope, your joy, and your all–in–all lies. You won't give up that prayerful relationship for anything because you, my friend, will have, at long last, learned to love to pray! Hallelujah!

The title of this portion of our book are words I heard my mother speak to God many times during my eighteen years under her roof. I heard her speak them so many times that when she did, I would go off in a corner by myself and pray to God for her. She spoke those words at times when she was bothered about the rent being due or when the lights got cut off. Sometimes the lights got cut back on, and sometimes they did not. But through it all, I learned to be a praying child, and I am a praying adult today. I learned early on that God will hear prayer. I learned though that the answer to the problem I brought to Him was not always immediate, I learned that as long as I had told Him about it, the worry about the problem need not exist anymore.

"In Thee, Oh Lord, I put my trust." My Momma also said those words before every meal she ate. She taught me by example to persevere. She taught me that things would work out in God's time, not mine. She told me to hold on to His hand no matter what, and that is what I did as a child, and that is what I do as an adult. And while we are talking about the subject of favorite Scripture and how they help to sustain us,

Here are two more of mine:

Romans 8:28 says, "All things work together for good for those who love the Lord."

Romans 8:31 says, "If God be for us, then who can be against us?"

He has been faithful to me, y'all. Having said that, I will leave you with two small poems for your reading and inspiration.

In Thee, Oh Lord, I Put My Trust
A poem of praise to the GODHEAD
From a little speck of dust
In YOU, I put all my trust
To prosper and protect me
Wherever I am led.

Renewal
Prayer renews my strength
Day by day
As I struggle to walk in
This Christian way.
When you have been in
Prayerful contact with God
There is a serenity that holds you
No matter where your footsteps may trod.
–excerpt from *DEI Sub Numine Viget*

******

One Last Testimonial Prayer

Jehovah Jireh

"God will provide," is one of the things
I can attest to as His child.
He looked upon me with love and as such
I can attest to His lovingkindness very much
I am one of those fatherless ones that
He shielded and held tight within His clutch.
Held and shielded and allowed to blossom and grow
All because of the provisional love
From the God that I have come to know.

****

Listen to my testimonial prayer I felt the urge to pray one morning upon rising.

Today, I feel the need to acknowledge my Father because of all He has done in my life. Think back through your life about all your ups and downs and victories and misses. Then think about where you are in contentment in your life today. Then give Him praise.

Dear God, It's Me, Alma

Lord, it is Alma L. Carr-Jones, known to some as "Sister Alma." You shepherded me through my childhood days of losing my daddy by making me realize You loved me. You showed me in innumerable ways that You did. When my clothes weren't up to par, You were there to wrap me in the arms of Your love by telling me, "One day."

Get Yourself Up

When my classmates belittled me and called me names because I did not live in the best area in town, You gave me hope in my future. You had me to know that one day, You would raise me above the inconsequential chatter of those classmates. You had me to know that, though the world looked upon me as a nobody, You looked upon me with lovingkindness.

You made this little nobody feel cherished enough that I could stand in front of the class and recite whatever it was the teacher had assigned to us. You made people look past my ragged clothes, past the area of town I lived in, past the fact that I did not have a daddy in the house, past the fact that grass grew knee high in the summertime in our yard in the middle of the city of Memphis, past the fact that my clothes smelled like charcoal and paper in the wintertime because we had no lights, gas, and water in the house, past the fact that I had to haul water from my aunt's house in canisters to see the little soul nestled within those trappings. You wrapped me in the cloak of, "That's okay because you will have these things and more one day."
You raised me up past where men would have me stay and You put me in a place where I could work for You. I work from the mountain of perseverance and faith. You gave me that, Father and I thank You.

For all You have done for me, the blessings, the lessons, the care packages, the high school guidance counselor who saw something in me she liked, and other benefactors as well, I humbly thank You. Now, it is my time to tell the world about the God I serve as I shine from the top of my mountain. All the glory belongs to You, O God. In the name of Jesus, I pray, Amen.

In Short

God is the only reason I made it this far. So, I will stand and tell the world I know that God will provide!

****

Finish Up

Remember, I had been wanting to be a teacher or a nurse since I was nine years old, but we had no money for me to go to college, and could see no way for it to happen, but I kept praying and believing and "Voilà!" I went!

I wanted to be a writer and "Voilà!" I am!

The one thing that has gone with me on all my travels in life is prayer. I have found that though situations change, and people change (come and go), God has been my constant, through prayer. Always BYDWP (Begin Your Day With Prayer.) I get up with Him in the mornings, and I take Him with me when I lie down to sleep at night. He still does that for me today.
What I am saying to you is that when you have to shed some tears, keep your hand in His hand, and everything will be all right. And whatever you do for the rest of your stay on this earth, don't ever quit praying because, as you can see, it works. Remember, "Faith retained – Blessings rain." I hope I fulfilled some need for you and that I gave you something to carry with you through your day and that the fervor I have used in my discussion about prayer has made you want to be in an intimate relationship with God, too, if you are not already.

(To the person who just thought, "Enough already, how many times are you going to say that to us?" My answer to you is, as

many times as is needed. I wanted to saturate your soul with it to the extent that you, too, will be thinking, "Let me see just what this God that she keeps going and on about is all about." Only then will my job for this lesson be done.)

I hope this treatise on prayer has strummed the chords of harmony and peace within your soul. And I further hope that when you are troubled in life, that you look back on this Scripture: *Romans 8:31. "What shall we then say to these things? If God be for us, who can be against us?" (KJV)* and all your worries cease.

This Scripture helps me a lot. You see, because I have such an intimate relationship with God, I know that whatever betides me, He will work it out for my good, so I "paint it green," (***Chopping My Row***, p. 21) pray, and keep on stepping. "Paint it Green" is my self-made slogan for meaning, "God is still in control."

There have been friends, colleagues, and enemies down through the years who have asked me or wondered how I made it through whatever it was I was going through at a given time in life and to all, I say once again, "By grace, through faith and prayer, God is the reason I made it."

Talked A Lot About Prayer

Talked so much about prayer because it is such an integral part of my life! I have seen it move mountains, shut down some enemies and make some others my footstool. You, my friend, need to make prayer a part of your arsenal of faith, if you have not already; then you, too, will become a strong proponent of prayer.

BYDWP

BYDWP
This is the essence of
MY faith, you see
Because no matter what disturbs my day
I always fall back on
The privilege I have to pray.
BYDWP
Is all I really need to say
Because there is no better way
To begin or end your day
Because BYDWP is the banner that
Has carried and sustained me
So, the last thought that I want
To leave with you about prayer is
BYDWP.

****

Your Story (Won't He Do It)

One day you will have a story to tell about how God answered your prayers. And I want you to bear the next two questions in mind. **1.** What did you do? **2.** Who did you tell, anybody at all? The words in the two preceding sentences seem to be a call for action. But what kind of action is called for and for what? The action called for refers to the title of this section, "Won't He Do It." The "He" referred to in the title is God. **This title asks all who have been on the receiving end of having prayers answered to "say so."**

Let the redeemed of the Lord tell their story – those He redeemed from the hand of the foe. (Psalms 107:2, NIV)

There is a popular song by Koryn Hawthorne, "Won't He Do It," where she expresses her praise to the Lord by song. That is what she did. And I tell mine every day on my blog and through my books. So again, the question to you is, "What do you do each day to let the world know about the awesome God you serve?"

If you are not an avid fan of talking to God yet, just give prayer a chance, you will be, because when you get answers to your prayers, you will want to include God in all your plans.

When you get your prayers answered, be sure to tell somebody! Folk need to hear your story just like you got reassurance from hearing mine. Let not what God has done for you become your best kept secret.

Answered prayers teach us a lot. They teach us to trust the Lord God's love and care for us. And when the answer is, "No," we learn, sometimes years later, that the Lord knew best back then as He does now. That knowledge helps to shore up our faith in Him. Throughout our lives, we continue to learn God's provision for us covers, not just the material aspects of our lives but every aspect.

What Else – Gratitude

So you won't be surprised when it happens to you, I will briefly mention "tears of gratitude." You see, what I only recently learned was that there would be times in my life when I would pray and shed tears of gratitude in praise. Now don't get me wrong, all of us, me included, have shed tears of gratitude in the immediate relief of the cessation of cataclysmic moments of destruction or near destruction. What I only very recently learned was that in moments of intense, introspective praise, when you approach the Master's throne, you will have gentle tears of gratitude and joy squeeze from between your lids and cascade down your cheeks as you commune with the Lord. Moments when you display yourself in all your vulnerability while acknowledging His supremacy and power and His beneficent intervention in your life. There have been times like that in my life, great and small and I thought I would share my perspective on tears of gratitude and praise with you. Hope you enjoy and that the following poem touches your soul with remembrances of His infinite, caring love.

Tears of Gratitude
I am not the first, and I won't be the last
But I just wanted to add my praise and
My gratitude to the trumpet's touting blast.
"When you get an answer, whether positive or negative
Don't forget to say, "Thank You"!
When you get an answer, don't forget to praise
As your arms and your voice to the throne
Of Jesus of Calvary, you raise."

Prayer has worked for me over the years, may you be blessed in your efforts, as well.

From the Ash Heap
"He raises the poor from the dust,
He lifts the needy from the ash heap
To make them sit with nobles,
And inherit a seat of honor;
For the pillars of the earth are the Lord's,
And He set the world on them." (1 Samuel 2:8, KJV)

Case in Point

Why is prayer such a vital part of my world?

Get Yourself Up

Jesus, prayer, and my Momma are the reason I made it out of the starting gate, down the long course, and am headed into the home stretch now. Let that rest upon your mind for a moment, if you will. You see, when I started life, it seemed I had a charmed course set for me. I was the little girl that my Momma had prayed so long for, and to boot, I was the apple of my daddy's eye. I was the baby, too. Now how much better can a start in life get? But life happened.

My daddy loved good times on the weekend, wine, and women more than he did his wife and family. And eventually, the inevitable happened, my parents separated, and I became the castoff who was petted too much by a daddy who was no longer in residence nor in attendance. I became known as the crybaby.

But I had a praying Momma who happened to be a preacher's daughter and that was my saving grace. I need to mention that I had a guardian angel I could see and talk to even before my daddy left. And even after I could no longer see him, I was still attended by forces of goodwill, it seemed.

After my Momma taught me about Jesus and the magic of prayer, and always being a deep thinker, I began to piece some of my life together. I knew things were going to happen before they ever did. I knew answers to questions that I could not tell how I knew them (junior high years). My mother often looked at me with a puzzled expression on her face as if she could not figure me out. She used to tell me that something had been trying to get my attention all my life. While I don't know about that, I do know certain people seemed to be drawn to me to want to help me and others took an almost instantaneous dislike to me (junior high years again).

I listened to the lessons taught to me by my Momma, my Sunday school teachers, the BTU teachers, and my teachers at school. I now know that I had what was almost a photographic memory but auditory. Anything I heard, I could play it back with precision just like a tape recorder. So when we took tests in elementary school and junior high school through, the seventh grade, at any rate, I aced them all.

And oh Lord, that is when I first encountered jealousy of a venomous sort and I did not have a daddy there to protect me, nor was I the teacher's pet anymore. I admit I encountered jealousy at home from my older brother, the middle child, and suffered some busted noses because of it, but that was nothing compared to the venom spouted toward me from some of my 7th–grade classmates. I don't guess I will ever forget the day that two of my most vocal haters got a group together and decided they were going to "cut my neck off." As was the custom back then, word spread among the other students that there was going to be a fight that particular afternoon.

I managed to tell my two brothers and they waited for me. As we walked toward home, a mob began to form. My brothers and I just kept walking. They were older than me by only a year and two, so they feared the mob, too. The mob surrounded us and the two girls who were the instigators stepped to the front. Y'all, I don't mind telling you that my teeth chattered, and my legs shook. What was my crime? I made straight A's that six weeks in school! That was it; that was what had that girl circling a razor around my neck. Straight A's! Umph. umph, umph!
I think I started hating my daddy from that point on. And I hated him through all my high school years, though I had relegated him to the back of my mind by then. I'll continue this story a little later in the book.

Get Yourself Up

Well, I think the fact that tears swam in my eyes may have softened the hearts of the fight mongers, I don't know. All I know is that my oldest brother said, "Come on, let's go," and we walked in a line pushing through the crowd that had us surrounded. It was my oldest brother, me in the middle, with my other brother bringing up the rear. I don't know how somebody managed to get between us, but they did and that is when I received a kick that I will remember as long as my brain cells work.

I can laugh about it now, but back then when I received that vicious kick square in my backside, it was not a laughing matter. I stumbled when they kicked me, but I never went down completely nor broke my stride. We kept walking with escape as our only goal.

The crowd soon dispersed since they realized there was not going to be an active fight because one of the people was a coward. Yes, that was me, folks. But you know, when I think back on my life now, I think there must have been ministering angels surrounding us that day because the young lady who had the razor was a tough customer who had moved in from a rougher neighborhood.

At any rate, Jesus brought me through with no lasting scars except on my mind and soul. And for a long time, I determined not to make straight A's again.

Yet, it was during those lonely junior high years I realized there was something different about me. It was during those years I started to know with regularity, what was going to happen before it actually did. I now know it was God's way of showing me I was not alone. It was His way of giving me hope for the dreary days that lay ahead of me. (You know, the charcoal bucket days and all mentioned in *Chopping My Row*.)

But things changed for me when I went to high school. I found friends I bonded with and I was not the smartest nor second smartest in my grade anymore. And that trigonometry, advanced math, and calculus was whipping me but good. I had to work hard at math and work hard, I did.

(Here is a side note: there was one subject in the mathematical field that I excelled in and you know what that was? Unified geometry! Yep, it was a series of theorems, postulates, axioms, and proofs. It was logical thinking and memory in total. So, of course, I excelled at it. My memory was excellent, and my deep thinking and reasoning skills were lifelong!)

Now I took the time to walk you through all that to say this. Just like Joseph, even in the worst times in your life, Jesus is right there, just like He was for Joseph and just like He was for me, even though Joseph could not see Him and neither could I. The fact remains that He had His angels down in the pit with Joseph when His brothers determined to kill him and also with him when Joseph was sold into Egypt and with him when he was in prison, and with him when Joseph was made second in command to all Egypt.

Joseph kept his faith in God and kept praying and doing the best he could in his situation. I did pretty much the same. I know that day in that wooded clearing when we were surrounded by those fight-lusting children that Jesus was right there with me. I kept my faith then and down through the years and have kept praying and waiting on Jesus through various phases of my life. AND He brought me through it all so I could tell this part of my story to you. Most of us have a story we can share about the presence of God and prayer in our lives; it just happened to be my turn to tell mine today.

So what we have to do is trust Him to take care of us in our needs. And how do we show Him and the world that we trust Him? By living a prayerful life is how. I have been walking with Him a long time and I treasure the relationship I have with Him! You know why, because there is no greater Friend.

God hears you when you pray and don't let anybody tell you differently! "God will work your trying situations out in such a way that the fact of His deliverance and provision will become your praise motto. "Oh, how awesome is our God!" *DEI Sub Numine Viget*

Poetry Offerings for Lesson 2

Telling My Story
He deserves my praise, and that is why
I sing His praise loud and long
And I will be singing them as
Long as my golden moments roll on.
If I can brag about the sports game and
Who Had the highest score
I can brag about the God of creation
Who made basketball, football, mankind
And so much more.
His wonders have made me
Open my mouth and made me shout
To tell this world what my God is about!
"You see, Y'all, I have a story that I want to tell
He snatched me from the clutches of hell
When I lost my way and from grace fell."

"Even now, He slaps back defeat and gives me victory
When the world thinks for sure, I am history
I can't explain it all, but it should be no surprise
That according to my worshipful eyes,
God Almighty is the most worthy topic
Proclaimed in both Biblical and secular history
For the Lord God is the architect of it all
The great Deliverer, Who answers when I call."

This poem is over, though I have not finished my story
But that would take too long because
I won't be finished until I open my eyes in glory.

Spirit Within

Sometimes thoughts just flow
As if they have a will of their own
As if they know the way to go
To reach the presence of the Holy One
But then, the Spirit dwells within
The hearts and minds of faithful men
To help us past some perilous zones
So that hope is not lost, and joy is not gone.

****

Not Alone

On this the next to the last day of February
I wanted to underscore the privilege
And the need we have in/for prayer
Yet, so often, we forget the love and the
Tenderness that waits with patience for us there.
Well, I will tell you as I have told so many before
I do not stress much about problems and situations
I just bow my knees to my Father and am troubled no more
Because while in attendance before His throne
He reassures me that I am His and that I am never alone.

****

A Prayer for You

Please intercede in the lives of my
Readers who have requested prayer
Please heal their bodies, minds
Heartaches, and griefs that they bear.
Bless each of them with the blessings
In which they stand in need
And let the fire of your love ignite
In them and their families

And in everyone that they meet.
– In Jesus' name, Amen.

****

A Prayerful Sunday
Today is the Lord's Day
And I know what I am going to do
I am going to attend worship and pray
And praise and thank Him for all
That He has brought me through.
And while I am there, I am going
To pray for our leaders and for our country, too
And pray hard for world peace
And for all the war talk rhetoric to cease.
Going to pray that hate be harnessed
And that the seeds of love be released
And carried far and wide
To take root in the soil of human souls
So that malice, envy, strife, and hatred
No longer exist to give birth to cruelty
Mass killings and such like
Gonna pray that this world's leaders
Be given a ride on the rails of peace
And that they are no longer governed by nationalistic pride
But governed, instead, by love for all humanity
For which the Savior died.
And one last thing, I'm sharing this prayer with you
In hopes that you will join hands with me
As we collectively knock on Heaven's doors
And push our urgent but humble prayer through.
"Father, heal our nation and heal our land
Because You are faithful, Father, and we know that You can."

Discussion Questions

1. Do you get a sense of welcome from Hebrews 4:16? Why?

_____

_____

_____

_____

2. What are the prerequisites listed for prayer listed in 2 Chronicles 7:14?

_____

_____

_____

_____

3. What happened in Acts 16:25–34 that had to do with answered prayer?

_____

_____

_____

_____

4. In Acts 12:1–17, why was Peter in prison in the first place?

_____

_____

_____

_____

5. How can you develop that "peace that surpasseth all understanding?"

_____

_____

_____

What Do You Think?

Why is it important to begin your day with prayer?

_____

_____

_____

_____

_____

_____

_____

_____

Further Reading
James 5:16; Romans 8:26

Presence of God
From the babble of a flowing brook
To a waterfall that cascades with its thunderous roar
I see the presence of God
In every place that I look.

10/10/21

Lesson 3:

The Water Cycle
(Soaring Above the Clouds)

Scripture: 1 Peter 4:12–14; Hebrews 13:5; Psalm 107; Hebrew 4:16

Aim: TO BE MINDFUL OF THE FACT THAT GOD ever welcomes us to His throne. TO REALIZE THAT, just as the earth is never without water, though there be seasons of drought or deluge, we are never alone. TO BE MINDFUL OF THE FACT THAT there is something in the rain, though sometimes we have to learn to skip in it.

Song: Hold on to My Faith

Hello there, fellow traveler through this land of time! [*Remember to BYDWP (begin your day with prayer), like I always advocate because when you do, you welcome the Lord's presence into all that your day may bring.*]

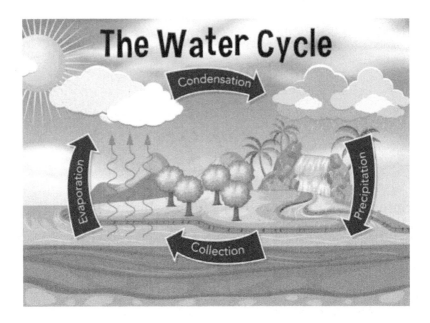

When you look at the picture of the water cycle above, you can see the continuity of the usage of water in the plan for the earth. The picture got me to thinking about water and its usage. So, when we get to our cases in point for the day, I will be using water in the application to life.

I find in life that things happen in cycles. That is the way God planned it. I mean, think about it. The seasons come in cycles over and over again throughout our lifetime, as does the cycle of populating the earth with people and animals. Now you take the rain, which is an integral part of the water cycle, as you can see in the illustration above.

Explanation – Here We Go
Physical Rain

As you can see from the illustration at the beginning of the lesson, rain or snow falling to the earth is called precipitation. As the rain falls it waters everything, flowers, trees, etc. It also collects in lakes, rivers, and seas, where some of it evaporates (changes into a gas) and rises back to the sky. Once there, it condenses (forms water droplets) and falls back to the earth again. This is a cycle that has been put in place by God for the watering and sustaining of the earth.

The illustration above that I gave you is of gentle rain, but we know all rain is not that gentle. It varies in intensity. But it serves a useful purpose because it sustains life.

God sends the physical rain for the betterment of the soil, flowers, trees, etc. And yes, He sends the physical rain to benefit us, too.

Walking by Faith: Spiritual Rain

Now about the spiritual rainy season or storm season in your life, there is a purpose for that, also.

Somebody might say, "Well, since He sees that I am out here working for Him, He ought to make the rain come later, or the storms completely go away or never arise in the first place." Tsk, tsk, tsk! The Bible says that everything happens for a reason. Read Hebrews 12:11 and take solace from that verse. You cannot do God's work if you are not properly trained and what better training can you get than from God?!

It causes us to thrive and grow into full–grown and strong servants of God. (1 Peter 4:12–14)

Read the 107th division of Psalms. You'll find that certain verses jump out at you. In my Bible, the subtopic of that chapter is entitled, "The Lord Delivers Men from Manifold Troubles."

Don't Let Go of Your Faith

My Momma told me that I "would"
I taught my school children that they "could"
These are the reasons that I am committed
To the book that you are now reading.
I had to show my children that "Being resilient
And holding on to a dream that might seem far away
Might turn out to be your saving grace one day."
It was not just something that I touted to sound good
But was something to be cherished and used
To hold on to dreams and bring about good.
As for my Mother, she taught me to always
Prepare for the unexpected situation that
Often crops up in life
To have a contingency plan that I entitled "Just in Case"
Thereby saving myself undue worry, strain, and strife.

****

But sometimes all the contingency plans in the world cannot prepare you. There are times when you simply must place your problems in the hands of Somebody bigger than you. That Somebody for me is the Lord God. When I look back on all the times He has brought me through I know I can lean on Him now. He has taken care of me all my life and I believe He will take care of me still. Why? He does so because I am His child, and He loves me. Yes, He loves you, too.

When troubles crop up in your life, it is all part of a cycle just like the rain. And remember the One Who orchestrated the cycles in the first place has carried you thus far. So, hold on, and trust in Him in all that you do.

When you are wrestling with troubles (rainy seasons), you get the world's attention like never before. They used to watch you with great envy as you walked and talked like a Christian ought to. Now, they watch you with glee because of the rain in your life. Some of them watch until they almost feel sorry for you, almost.

Now, Here's the Ticket

What kind of show are you giving them to watch? Is it a show of faith or a show of complaining about the injustice that is heaped upon you? If you complain, then your enemies and the adversary get the glory. But oh, if you remain steadfast in your faith with a smile painted on your face even though pain and tears may, at times, shimmer in your eyes, all the glory goes to God! (1 Peter 4:12–14, KJV) And, as I said earlier, some of your enemies may develop a grudging admiration for you. Uhmm, I said might.

More than likely, though, they may never tell you, even if they discuss it among themselves.

But Just Think About It

Your rainy season is causing God to get the glory, and you have commanded your enemies' admiration. And it might be to the extent that they begin to wonder about this faith you have and about this God you serve. Some might wonder enough to ask. Glory to God! *(That thought might have you skipping through the rain in your life.)*

But even though you have gained the admiration of some of your enemies, you still think that this storm of yours is unfair and not right, huh? Well, remember what the Lord told Job in Chapter 40, verse 1? And I am paraphrasing:

"Oh! So, you, faultfinder, are going to contend with God Almighty so you can be justified? Can the thing that was created correct the Creator?"

Trust Him and Don't Question
There is something in the rain
There is a good reason for all my pain.
(Hebrews 12:11)

And the Rain Keeps Falling

Drip, drop, drip, drop, drip, drip, drip … What do you do? Not only are your enemies looking, but so are other Christians and God, too. You might feel like it is a bit too much and like you cannot make it. I understand because I have been there and done that. But I had to remember, and you do too, that according to Hebrews 11:6 and Ephesians 5:10, you must have faith to please God. And remember that He will never leave us nor forsake us. (Hebrews 13:5, KJV)

Look at the words to these two poems and remember that you may damage or strengthen somebody's faith in God by the way you handle your rainy season. That's why I advocate learning to skip in the rain.

Think You Can't Make It
So, you think you can't make it
I tell you that is just not so
Listen to me brother or sister of mine
And I will tell you what I know. *(Chopping My Row, p. 22)*

Must Remember
Must remember that people are watching me
As I travel along life's highway.
Must remember that I might influence someone
By what I do and what I say *(Chopping My Row, p. 25)*
So, you may
See me skipping as I go on my rainy way.

****

In the meantime, if you will go back and look at Psalm 107, you will see that the entire chapter talks about God's deliverance of His children from trouble. And, too, notice that the chapter both begins and ends with giving thanks to God for His lovingkindness. This means we ought to tell somebody about the goodness and love of God.

If He has provided for you, you ought to tell somebody. If He has made a way when you were backed against the wall and saw no way out, you ought to tell somebody.

The first two verses in Psalm 107 say that those who know the Lord should tell of His goodness. That is what it means when it says, "Let the redeemed of the Lord say so." (Psalms 107:1) And the last verse in the chapter tells you to think about these things. What things – the way He always provides because of His lovingkindness, always!

That means that in whatever way you have a need, He has you covered. He is so good, y'all and I am glad He loves us. Aren't you?

That's why I can skip in the rain of life sometimes, when it seems that I ought to be shut down with sadness and disappointment.

I told you earlier, when we discussed the water cycle that the water comes in different forms, some more noticeable than others. We learned that water is always present in the atmosphere, but rain is the most noticed and familiar.

Now, let's talk a little more about the rainy season in a Christian's life. We have already established the fact that it comes in cycles, as well. Our parents, elders, etc. sought to prepare us and equip us for the rainy seasons that were sure to be a part of our lives.

When you look at the way they trained us, you can see we were taught early on in life to pray to God (reliance on God). We were given that introduction to the Lord in special ways.

Most of us learned to give thanks to the Lord before we could talk properly. Remember food blessings such as:

> Thank You for the world so sweet
> Thank You for the food we eat
> Thank You for the birds that sing
> Thank You, dear God, for everything.
> Amen

or

> God is great
> God is good
> Lord, we thank You for our food.
> Amen

Remember the little nightly prayer we were taught?

Get Yourself Up

Now I lay me down to sleep
I pray the Lord, my soul, to keep
If I should die before I wake
I pray the Lord, my soul, to take.
Amen

I remember being taught to say, "The Lord's Prayer," each night before I went to sleep. We did not question it; the prayer was just a part of our nightly procedure for bedtime.

We learned prayers for waking each morning.

We were taught to praise the Lord, too. Remember having to commit to memory the 23rd Psalm and the 100 Psalm?

In essence, we were taught, "Ask God. Tell God. Praise God." And we did, too.

I remember being told that we, as children, were living our most carefree days. I thought that was as dumb as a box of rocks, at the time. But oh, now I understand! I have had some rainy seasons, some long nights, times in my life I felt I just could not take it anymore, times when people hated me just for being happy in Jesus, times that my enemies I had done nothing to, dug ditches for me because they felt like I should not be able to do the things I was able to do. Yet, I remember when I did not know what a rainy day or season was!

But I know now and I know what to do when they come. Talk to God. Tell Him what the problem(s) is and keep my faith in Him while I wait, like Job said, "for my change to come."

I Remember

I remember hearing my Momma and some of the older church members sing about God making a way. I remember being taught the words to the song, "I Know the Lord Will Make a Way, Oh Yes He Will." When I read the entire 107th division of Psalms, I see a beneficent Father watching over His children, of which I am one.

In the 107th division of Psalms, I can see:

1. The children being in trouble,
2. Them praying to God and asking for deliverance,
3. God delivering them
4. Them thanking God for delivering them,
5. Them telling the world about what the Lord has done for them in their trouble and what He can do for all who are His. I see them bragging on God and I know from reading this passage of Scripture that the Lord is pleased by their bragging on Him. (We are told in Jeremiah 9:24 that God likes for us to brag on Him.)

The list of five things presented above is what I call "The Christian's Storm Cycle."

Now that I have presented my explanation of the rainy season in a Christian's life to you, I will give you some explanatory examples I have experienced in my life.

Be That As It May
Be that as it may
I looked the situation over
And thought, "Not today!"

The verse above could have been taken from someone's life who has had enough! There are negative situations that crop up spasmodically in our lives that threaten to shred our last vestige of peace. Then there are those negative situations that are ongoing with waves of intensity that ebb and flow. After you tell God about your problems, ask Him for help.

Here's the thing. Strive to remain calm in tumultuous situations by:

- prayerfully remembering Whose child you are
- walking away
- reading the Bible
- reading a funny book
- engaging in an enjoyable hobby
- remembering that this, too, shall pass
- repeating to yourself a verse or saying that gives you strength such as, "I still trust in You, Lord." (Read Job 13:15)
- Remembering the times before that He brought you through and praising Him while you wait.
- And always remember that the church of tomorrow watches you today.

Be patient with your situation while you learn all you can from it.

You never know when you may be called upon to share the lessons you learned.

And remember that if the rain lasts long enough, you gain strength by weathering its falling (Hebrews 12:11).

<u>Case in Point</u> – Examples

Examples or testimonies of how, through His lovingkindness, God will provide. I hope you will enjoy them and be blessed by the telling.

This is the first one of my rainy seasons I want to share with you. I am going to take these excerpts from my book, ***Chopping My Row***.

"One day my husband came home to make the grand announcement that he had gotten us cheaper insurance. Ever mindful of saving money I said, "Good." Then he said to me in a sort of hesitant way, 'Uh, there is just one problem.' I was busy cooking dinner, so I absent–mindedly asked, 'What?' He said, 'Well, the policy we have lapses on this date, but our new insurance does not pick up until a week later.' I almost came unglued. I whipped out, 'You mean to tell me that we will be without insurance for a whole week?!'

Y'all, he must have been practicing for telling me because he yelled out, 'Hold it! Just one minute! We have had insurance for years and not once have we needed it! Just what do you imagine is going to happen in one week.?' Folks, he was so irate, and I realized that we had not ever used our renter's insurance. Still, I knew that I would be on pins and needles for the entire week. Guess what happened during the **one** week when the grace period of the old policy lapsed and the new one had not yet kicked in? Yep, you guessed it.

On April 16, 1987, my house burned down to the ground! The fire was so hot it even burned up the floor. If you have never experienced a house fire, you have no true idea of the trauma it wreaks on your life. It will attack you in ways that you never even thought about. It will shake your faith to the core. You will find you miss things taken for granted such as your children's baby pictures. You will think about them and cry. But then you will remember the Scripture Job 14:14.

Remember when I told you to always look for your blessing in your storm? Uhm Hmm–m.

Job 14:14 is a good reference Scripture for that. Read it. Start thinking about what possible good can come out of the chaos or trouble in which you find yourself. Now, here are the blessings from my house fire, some of which I realized then and others years later.

There was no loss of life in the fire. My babies had been at school and my husband had been at work and I had been in my classroom teaching.

My mother, bless her heart, had been the only one at home at the time of the fire and she had the tip end of one of her plaits burned off and that is all. When I got to my house that day, she was standing across the road from the blazing house along with some of the other neighbors looking dazed as if she could not believe this had happened. She had not been cooking anything, but the fire had already burned her house to the ground and was well on its ways to devouring mine. But she was okay! I got to have my Momma for 17 more blessed years. When she did die, I realized what the Lord had not allowed the fire to take from me that April 16th day. (Her leaving me is a narrative for another day but suffice it to say I did not know anything could hurt that badly.)

I had a cat I kept in the house and it got some scorched paws and had to spend a couple of days at the vet but it was okay too. It lived to a ripe old age after the fire.

I vowed to use my china if I ever got any more and not have it sitting up in the china cabinet waiting for some special occasion or for my new house.

All my kid's pictures that I had cried so over, were delivered to me by various family members and friends I had given copies of them to.

We are insurance poor, nowadays.

Have had several riding mowers since then.

The kid's schools supplied them with new bikes and clothes.

My school took care of my clothes, and the kitchen, and got me that precious broom that I had cried so over. As a matter of fact, I received three brooms. (tee hee)

Church members, black and white (a lesson in that for us today), supplied everything else. And I do mean everything else. It was nothing for someone to walk up to me and ask what else I needed or for them to shake my hand and leave it graced with a hundred-dollar bill. I still have a mental picture of three church members bringing a brand new couch and armchair into my house. I never knew people could care so much. That outpouring of love across racial barriers put a smile on my face. I think it was God's way of sending me a care package, one of those tailor–made blessings that has your name written all over it. And I have never forgotten the feeling of receiving the gift. I also have never forgotten that people will look at you to see how you handle your adverse situation and that you might just bless somebody for a storm that is headed their way by your reaction to your own storm.

We stayed with my husband's aunt and uncle for two nights after the fire and then moved to a little yellow house on a hill in the heart of Martin. It even had a washing machine in it, not as nice as the one I had, but never–the–less, a washing machine.

My mother was given her own apartment, for which she was very thankful.

It taught me that people will look at you to see how you handle a situation in your "stress times." I repeated this one because I want you to be very aware of it. Our reactions do speak for or against the Lord. Because of the kindness of people, who here–to–fore had not been kind or had been nonchalant, a smile was put on my face. I found out later that smile of mine was seen by others as *skipping through the rain.*

Though I had lost everything I had worked for and built over 13 years, now all savings were gone; income tax money received the week before had been spent on new bicycles and new spring clothes for the kids and a riding lawnmower, but all had been taken away in a flash. I learned to lean on the Lord like I never had, and He brought me out. God showed me He could and would provide.

I was so surprised and overwhelmed by the goodness of people that I kept a smile on my face. I was amazed and touched that people were coming to me with love and comfort like we were brothers and sisters under God and not of different races. Even now, folks, I am touched by the outpouring of love we received during that time. And that smile I kept on my face was blessing someone in a mighty way, though I didn't know it at the time. I will share that story with you now.

Remember I told you I received another blessing from the storm of my house burning down to the ground with no insurance?

Well, here is what happened.

I told you about the lady who came to me with a compliment because of how my faith stayed strong during the time of my fire, you know, losing so much and with no insurance to boot. She thought it was outstanding that I could have a smile on my face during that time. She told me she wished she had a faith that strong. I thanked her and kept moving. Well, about seven to eight months later, this same lady was diagnosed with stage four cancer. She lived less than a year after her diagnosis. But she told me something I will remember as long as the Lord allows my thought processes to flow.

One day she said, "Alma, come here a minute, I want to talk to you. I just wanted to tell you, Alma, that I admire you. Yes, I know that shocks you, but I do. This is why I admire you. Back in the spring when your house burned, you kept a smile on your face. And now, I can have that same strong faith that you displayed. That is how I am making it through this cancer and the ravages it has put on my life and on my body. So Alma, I just wanted to say, 'Thank you.'"

Folks, I have never forgotten the lesson she taught me that day even though she did not realize she taught me one. And that is why you will often hear me say, be a blessing to someone else in their rainy season even though you are going through one of your own because, folks, we just don't know why we are going through what we go through. There are lessons and blessings in the *rain*.

There were two other times I used what I had learned in the fire to bless others who had been victims of losing their homes to fire.

Case in Point

Several years after my house fire, one of the teachers at my new school (out of Special Education and given a regular classroom by now) lost her home to a fire. Since the school where I was moved to was the one that had bought new clothes for my son and his new bike, they knew I had suffered a fire two years back.

Therefore, they came to me with a request that I list some of the things that would be needed in a fire. I listed what I thought was needed, but I reiterated, again and again, the need to go to her when they went to her house with a broom. Most of them scoffed at the idea and would not do it. They took all kinds of things, big and little. When they got to her, she was overwhelmed with thanks and burst out crying saying, guess what? You got it, "But I don't even have a broom straw!" They sent some of the men pronto to get that broom and a mop and a dustpan, etc. They all said, "She said to get a broom," meaning me.

Now, how did I know to tell them that, hmm–mm?

Case in Point

I had a closer friend than the one mentioned above to lose half of her home to fire, but she had insurance. Her needs were slightly different from what I felt at the time of my fire. She did not lament about not having a broom straw. Instead, she lamented about her kids' pictures that had so much smoke and water damage as she stood in the rain and cried. Her fire happened in the spring just as mine did and I will never forget standing in light misting rain and listening to her talk about how lost she felt.

Y'all, her pain was so deep it stirred the embers of how I felt when I experienced my fire. I looked at her and I said, "I know you don't understand, and I bet you wonder why the rain keeps falling and the wind is still blowing like everything is all right in the world, don't you?" She said, "Yes! But it is not all right! My world had taken a big hit and things are not normal and right!"

I looked at her and said, "I want you to listen to me really hard right now. I know you feel pain over the loss of some of your kids' pictures, but at least you have some to sort through and lay out to dry to see what is left. When I had my fire, I cried because they were all burned up. I did not know it at the time, but family members I had given copies of their pictures to were, even before the fire got cold, going through their pictures, and getting me ones of my children.

You see, God was remembering me even then and you are wondering how God could allow this to happen to you after all you have tried to do for Him, aren't you?"

She broke down even more and sobbed, "Yes!" Then I said, "I know how you feel, but listen to this. We are standing in the misty rain, aren't we?" She nodded her head, yes. Then I said, "You said earlier, 'How can the rain still be misting like everything is all right,' didn't you?" Again, she nodded her head, yes. I pointed to the ground and said, "Look at the water that has just fallen to the ground. Do you see what it is doing? It is rolling on down the driveway to the drainage ditch you have. But it doesn't stop there because the drainage ditch is carrying it on down to the creek at the end of the road. But it doesn't stop there either. That creek flows on down to the river which in turn empties into a larger river which in turn empties into the ocean somewhere.

Now, that says to me since these things were put in place by God and they are still functioning, doing what He intended for them to do when He created them, that God is still in control. That is why the wind keeps gently blowing and the rain keeps misting. It is telling you that God is still in control." In other words, folks, that water cycle was still operating just as it did in the beginning.

She grabbed my neck and cried in earnest then. She said, "Oh Alma, that is so beautiful. I will never look at my fire in the same way again. Thank you." She said, "It still hurts, but I can take it better now because you changed my perspective. You made me see that, in even this, my Father, is still mindful of this world and me. He sent you, Alma, and you gave me just the words I needed to hear. Thank you!"

Folks, I did not miss a beat. I told her that one day she might be called upon to help someone else through the trauma of a house fire and that because of her pain, she could help others negotiate through theirs. Now, I would not have known what to tell any of the people who experienced fires if I had not suffered a fire of my own.

But I can tell you this, if you have the chance to take something to the victim of a house fire if that victim is a woman and especially if there is no insurance, I strongly suggest that one of the things you her take is a broom. There is just something about the broom. (If you do not understand the broom association, be thankful and hope that you never do.)

Yes, I used the lessons I learned through the trauma of my house fire to comfort others who were in a rainy season of their own. This is one of the ways I can add my voice to the crowd of witnesses that says, "God will provide." I can say that because I am a living witness that whether you need food, clothes, shelter, kind words and/or an understanding ear, He sends it all.

God Will Provide
I am one of the redeemed of the Lord
And I am saying that God will provide
Thus I am so proud that He walks by my side.

****

For the record:
Not everyone who has a storm
Has it because of their sin
Sometimes a storm is sent because
Of the multiplicity of lessons found therein.

****

Why am I taking the time to explain all this? It's simple, folks, because I am one of the redeemed, I care about you and about your relationship to the God of Heaven. And there may be someone who needs to hear these words. The last verse in Psalm 107 reminds us to "think on these things."

We are going to have rainy seasons in life. That is a given fact. How you handle them can draw or drive people to the Lord. We have just finished doing a rather lengthy study of Psalm 107. In it, we saw a cycle that occurs over and over in the life of a

Christian. The cycle goes as such:

- We are a praying people of faith and, as such, when trouble arises in our lives, we tell God.
- God answers our prayers.
- We give heartfelt and grateful thanks and share the news of what a Deliverer the God we serve is. Yes, in essence, we brag on God. *(The Christian's Storm Cycle)*

We often have a respite from rainy cycles, but they will come time and time again because of the very nature of life. It was noted earlier that we are in one of three positions when it comes to storms or rainy days in our lives, we are in the midst of a rainy season, we just got out of one or we are just getting ready to go into one. The thing we must strive to remember is that through it all, give God glory and remember He sees, He knows, and He cares.

Go with me to our God's throne as we speak to Him concerning the rainy days we have in our lives.

"Owing to your faithfulness FATHER, we know that everything in our lives is going to be okay because You have already told us so in Your Word. We have just finished reading from the book of Job, Chapter 38 and from the book of Psalms, Chapter 107. So for the times, as now or recently, that we have the thought in our minds, 'This isn't fair what's happening to me … But I didn't do anything.' We repent FATHER. We are so sorry and ask YOU to forgive us. You see FATHER, we forgot to remember:

- that though it is hard right now, it is still not the "charcoal bucket days;" (pages 104-105, **Chopping My Row**)

- that ultimately, everything that happens in our lives, YOU have control of. We also know that when Job was going through what he was going through, nothing could happen to him without YOUR say so. YOU limited how much the adversary could do to him just like You limit how much turmoil the adversary can inflict upon us.
- I also know that YOU brought Job through okay.
- But You didn't stop there. Just like a mother who prepares for a new baby gets things ready, You, in all Your wisdom, built in hope for us when You had Job's story recorded, Psalm 107 and in fact the whole Bible. You have shown Your love in everything You have done for us, especially through Your Son, Jesus.
- You, not only, had the Bible written for us but then You had the Scriptures themselves tell us they contain "Everything that pertains to life and godliness." And then You had it further to say that "Whatsoever things that were written before time were written for our learning." It is no coincidence that there are examples and stories for us in the Bible, the book, that we go to often for encouragement and spiritual nourishment because You had the Bible prepared for us with love. I am proud to be living during the time of free Bible reading and in a country where there is no penalty of death due to exercising our right to serve You.

Thank You, Father and forgive me when I complain about the storms/rainy seasons in my life. I will keep reminding myself of all the preparations that You have made for and continue to make for me, and I will keep saying, "I don't believe You brought me this far to leave me because, God, You have shown me that You have and will continue to provide for me." I love You. It is in Jesus' name, I pray, Amen. (*Chopping My Row*, pages 28–29)

Get Yourself Up

If you have ever had a time in your life when you thought, "What am I going to do now?" you understand what I was talking about in the lesson today. If you are having a moment such as that right now, then this lesson was written for you.

Remember there is a bright side somewhere. Sometimes you must keep looking to see. When the storm is raging, you reflect upon things that are most important and if the storm lasts long enough you are forever changed, in that those things you value then become your norm.

You can liken it to cataract surgery. You see life through a cloud of bad habits, decisions, etc., but after the surgery you see so much clearer. Just as it took the surgery to clean up your vision often it takes a storm to help us clean up our lives to see better.

After the rainy season is over, we walk with renewed purpose, surer steps, and a clearer focus. And we do it all, because we kept the faith and kept looking for a better day. So, whatever you do, keep looking, my friends, and you will be blessed.

Oh, Storm, What Art Thou

Oh, storm, what art thou
But a venue for God to show
Forth His peaceful love and care
Oh, storm, what art thou
But a monstrous conflagration of circumstance
That builds a song of grateful safety
And makes my voice swell in grateful praise
To the great God, Who orders my steps
And guards me in all my ways
And is always listening up there

To my dependent and sincere prayer
Oh, storm what art thou
Naught!

****

Life happens, but if we are persistent enough, we usually get things done.

We must take things one day at a time. That is like taking one step at a time. How are mountains climbed, one step at a time, right? Then you and I must do the same thing with those pesky life situations that threaten our joy.

In the storm, keep a praying faith. After the storm remember Who bought you through it and share the news with your fellowman after giving thanks for your deliverance. Put the deliverance in your arsenal of faith for future use when you enter the rainy season again because you remember that life goes in cycles.

Case in Point

For the Newbies – To Help Get You Prepared

I wanted to talk to those of you who have not been hit by life and don't know about feeling like you have had enough of rainy days for a while.

So, I want to take you on a "What if" scenario trip. A scenario that will help you during those times when you feel you have been in the storm too long. Ready? Let's go.

Get Yourself Up

Do you remember when you got your first place of your own? Nothing quite like that feeling, is there? You felt like the whole world was out there waiting for you to make your mark upon it. You felt invincible, didn't you?

Yep, there was nothing you could not achieve. Finally, you were an adult and out of trade school or college and ready to start living the life you had planned since you were a kid. Ah–h, remember that carefree feeling, that feeling of invincibility?

Hmph, then life had a go at you. But you were optimistic and weathered most of your storms, which seemed minimal at first. There were ups and downs through the years, but you persisted.

You kept going. No matter what happened, you kept your faith in the God your mother had talked to you so much about. Yes, that same God you talked to so much as a child and learned to lean on and trust, kept you going through the good times and through the rough times.

You learned to bend without breaking, and in general, to be flexible. You learned to trust in God to help you make it through. People began to marvel at your faith, and you, you kept moving doggedly forward, your only goal to make it to Jesus and Heaven. Somehow, determination, grit, and persistence had become your allies.

You did well. You learned to take life one day at a time. You learned to climb the mountain you were on, one small step at a time… And then, one day you awoke with the knowledge that you had reached the top of the mountain whose rough side you had been climbing for years. You awoke to know, just know, that things were going to be different. You didn't know how you knew, and you didn't care. You just knew that your years in the rainy season and the climbing of that mountain were over.

Now, with that scenario over, how do you feel? Do you feel exhilaration, relief? You feel like that because of a "what if" scenario we walked through today. Then here is what I want you to do for each day of your life for the rest of your life whenever you are in a rainy season. With each new day, hope that today might be the day your rainy season ceases. And then, my friend, you step on, because one day your rainy season will end, and perpetual joy will begin. One day your happiness will be so great you will scarce think it is real.

Just Think About It

How do you think Job felt when his captivity was turned? Such joy, oh such joy! And you too, my friend, if you remain faithful. You, too!

Be blessed today, y'all and know that all rainy seasons eventually pass and that lessons and blessings from them will linger on to say, "God will Provide!" And never forget that Our Father is always listening, looking, and ever caring and waits for us to approach His throne, to which, He has given us a warm invitation. *(Hebrews 4:16, KJV)*

<u>Case in Point</u>

When life gets you over a barrel, and things are extraordinarily rough, that is the time your enemies love to talk about you and ask one question about you and, some of them, to you, "Where is his/your God?" (Psalm42:3) That is the time when you need to shine the most for Him. Even though your heart may quail within you, you let that person or persons know, just like Job did, that your faith in God is still intact. That is the time you open your mouth as say like Job said in Job 13:15, "Though He slay me, yet will I trust in Him."

Then you say to yourself,
> "Why are you depressed, O my soul?
> Why are you upset?
> Wait for God!
> For I will again give thanks to my God for his saving intervention." *(Psalm 42:5, New English Translation)*

Similar words are penned in Psalms 42:11. You can go on to say to them, "God's favor lasts a lifetime. "(Psalms 30:5, KJV) And I know that if I wait on Him, He will deliver me. Blessed be the name of the Lord." 1Peter 5:10.

You see I heard about Him from my mother and those gone on before me, and I learned about Him through experience, myself (Psalm 48:8, KJV) and that is why I can tell you, like David said in the 48th division of Psalms:

For such is God (God is faithful) and He will guide us until death.

And until then, I will wait patiently for the Lord. (Psalms 40:1, NASB) He put me on top once: He can do it again.
I wait patiently on the Lord because I delight to do His will. (Psalms 40:8, NASB)

As I have often told you before, this race I run is not about me, it is about getting the work of the Lord done according to His will as I work my way toward eternity. It's that simple. It's that sweet!

Read Psalms 40:5 and you will understand why I keep talking about God. He is awesome in all that He does, and I want the world to know what a precious gift we have been given through Jesus in being allowed to serve God. How excellent is His name in all the earth!

Look at what God did for me during my rainy season while I was waiting on Him!

See the great book reviews He gave me?

Reviews of *Chopping My Row*

- Get on the Next Book!
- You and God sit down and talk about it. Wow, Sis. I know you had that little talk with Jesus. Amen and God bless! ~ Reader of *Chopping My Row*

By a Phone Call

I received a phone call one night and the dear lady who called me said she called me expressly to tell me that my latest book was phenomenal! You know that I have already been told by someone else that they thought that, *Chopping My Row* was phenomenal. And now, another one! Wow, all I can say is that God is good! So I posted a Thank You on Facebook for the great reviews; here's what I wrote:

"It is such a joy to be able to write about my God and to have people say the book is phenomenal. But I tell people the phenomenal One is God because He gave the book to me and I thank Him for allowing me to serve. Y'all be blessed. My heart is full so all I can say is, "God's grace!""

Here are some more responses I got to my post concerning my book, ***Chopping My Row***:

- Alma, where can I buy your book??!!

- We are waiting for the next BOOK!!!!

- I could hear your voice as I read this – like you were right here in the room. You go, precious lady!

- But God . . .

- "I would love to share something with FB family & friends, I purchased a book ***Chopping My Row*** by Sister Alma L. Jones. That book is inspirational & overwhelmed, I spoke to sister Alma Louise Jones to let her know how much I was inspired by her book, Thru GOD'S strength she nailed it. WOW & I MEAN WOW.

  Then in lesson 2 "Shelter in the Time of a Storm" Awesome, it sent chills up & down my back, phenomenal I know I probably didn't spell it well. Even though I only made it to page 59, you need to purchase this book it's worth it ***Chopping My Row*** by Sister Alma L. Jones.

- Sister Jones, I sincerely want to thank you for that phenomenal book. Now, I said before I'm not a book reader, so you know when you get my attention to read a book, nobody but God – God gave you your calling, and He did it well. Chapter Two – Shelter in the Times of the Storm. WOWWWWW." Deborah S.

- This is the only spiritual book that I have read. Though I have never chopped any cotton, I felt like I was in the midst of every event that took place. The book is written where anyone can read and understand. I purchased 6 more for my family members and to donate to centers. It is a guaranteed read. Thanks, Ms. Alma for what you do for everybody and how you share your gift from God!!! May He continue to bless you!! Deborah, Amazon Customer

- A great spiritual read!

- I really enjoyed this book and would recommend it to anyone who is trying to live a spiritual life. It would be great to use for a women's study group. Donna, Amazon Customer

- America Needs this Book!

- As a Christian and avid reader, this book, *Chopping My Row* contains Biblical jewels and insights of living for Jesus everyday! As a Christian chops his or her row everyday we become encouraged and stronger in our faith and witness! Ms. Jones is a realistic and informative writer and keeps you thinking about your life and how to improve your walk with Christ every day! America needs this book and how to have a great revival, in order to turn this nation back to God! Larry, Amazon Customer

- Such a Great Read!
- This is such a great read and perfect for women who are wanting fain more insight for their spiritual walk. I highly recommend this book!

Case in Point

I think for our final *case in point* today I will address the subject of Soaring Above the Clouds. "What made me come up with the topic of 'Soaring above the Clouds,' somebody asked. One of the things that you might think is flying on an airplane. And that is a good place to start. But you know me, I take it further in my thinking than flying on a literal plane.

So, in delving into the topic of Soaring Above the Clouds, did you know the earth is approximately 70% water? Yep, it surely is! And did you further know that you are approximately 70% water? Yep, you are. Look it up if you find that hard to believe. That is what I did when I first heard about the earth and us being 70% water.

If you take the time to look it up, you will see the approximate number of 70% is correct. And then if you think a bit more, you might think that God made the earth and made us too.

Now, I do not know about you, but the next thing I think is, "No wonder He could walk on water when He was here on earth; no wonder He could change water into wine; no wonder He sent the Israelites through the Red Sea on dry land bordered by two walls of water; no wonder He went back to Heaven on a cloud and no wonder He will come back the same way!" I say, "No wonder!" but you know that means I am agog at the piece of information I just put together in a moment of epiphany.

Water is one of the elements and He seems to be partial to working with it. Granted, He can control all the elements and we have been shown this via the Bible. But my fascination today is on the water element since we are talking about the water cycle.

Bringing It Home

Some of you are well ahead of me in this line of thinking, and others of you are still scratching your head. Okay, let me lay it out for you, filet it so to speak. What are clouds made of, water vapor, right? Jesus used one as an elevator to go back to Heaven, didn't He? He will take that elevator back to earth one day to gather His own, right? That means you and me. Which means that one day, I am going to get to ride the cloud back to glory with my Lord and Savior, Jesus.

Y'all, do you get my drift?

Remember, Peter asked the Lord if he could walk on the water and he was granted that request until his faith failed him. But you and I can ride on water when we take that elevator back to Heaven with Jesus if we keep our faith intact.

Yes, one day we will get to go back home with Him, and we will be doing more than soaring above the clouds. We will be navigating the clouds via Jesus!

So, when I was on the airplane en route from a recent trip to California, where I had been visiting my grandbaby, I thought about Jesus and I wondered how His trip up through the clouds via a cloud felt.

I could hear the motor of the airplane, and I knew that God's giving man the technology of airplanes was the way we could move as fast and as safely as we did through the sky. Yes, I knew it was His grace that kept us aloft because, unlike the bird, He did not give us wings to fly. Yet by His grace, I was able to soar above the clouds and move at record time.

And right on the hills of that thought came the one that said, one day, He's coming back, and all the saints are going to be caught up with Him and, y'all, we will ride that majestic elevator home to glory as we soar above the clouds. How grand and how sweet and oh, how wonderful!

I will tell you this, my joy will be greater than the Snoopy character that I put on my Twitter feed on Sunday, November 17, 2019; in fact, it will be the greatest joy that I have ever known!

Yes, we will soar above the clouds and won't need any motor to hold us up because we will be lighter than water vapor and the Shepherd, Himself, will be herding His sheep home! Hallelujah!

Poetry Offerings for Lesson 3

Well, Well, Well

There are times that bring life changing catastrophic news
That seems to stroll with leisure through your life
Often taking up residence, it seems
Then there are happy times that are so fleeting
That you wonder if and when there'll be another meeting.
But what can always be counted on is
The fact that nothing lasts forever whether good or bad
And you have to learn to make the most of the good times
And ride out the ones that make you sad.
So, savor the good times and make sweet memories
That will help you through when you have those times that
Make you shake your head and say
"Well, well, well," or "Umph, Umph, Umph."
— Always remember that these, too, shall pass away.

****

Keep looking and you will see
The blessing in the storm that attends thee
For out of every storm there are lessons learned
As pruning is done and the debris of bad habits
Is collected and burned.

****

**When I don't understand,
I have a loving God Who does and
For Him I have taken my stand.**

My Stand
When the storms rise
And the winds blow
You are in the hands of God Almighty
You know.

You are in His hands
And He can do with you what He will
He can allow the storm to keep raging
Or He can order peace to be still.
Whatever He decides at any given point in time
Just remember that He cares for you,
That your troubles have no hiding place
And that some faltering soul may be watching you
As you stand your ground and continue your race.
At the end of my journey, I may
Present a soul that is battle scarred
From the skirmishes by which
My faith has been marred
But I will wear a victorious smile that proclaims
"Here is a Christian deemed 4–Starred."

Discussion Questions

1. What Scripture tells us that we are welcome to the throne of God?

_____

_____

_____

_____

2. According to 1 Peter 4:12–14 how does the world view the fiery trials *(rainy seasons)* of a Christian?

_____

_____

_____

_____

3. How do we know, as Christians, that we are never alone?

_____

_____

_____

_____

4. What do verses 5 and 11 of Psalm 42 say that is similar?

_____

_____

_____

_____

What Do You Think?

What does soaring above the clouds in the title have reference to?

_____

_____

_____

_____

For Further Reading

Psalm 139:13–16

Sometimes we have to have faith as simple as a child.

My Best Friend
God is my best friend
With Jesus and the Holy Spirit
Who all send angels to see about me when
I feel bad and am sick and down
They make me feel better and take away my frown.©
–(written by Candace, my daughter)
****

Didn't Think That I Could Last
Didn't think that I could last
Through the storm and its furious blast
But when I remembered from my past
How the Lord had brought me through
With Masterly finesse and left me with
Aplomb that left my enemies envious and aghast
I determined to ride the tide
In that, the storm's fury could not last
Because Jehovah Nissi held me fast.

Lesson 4:

Help Is on the Way

Scripture: Job 23:10; Romans 5:3–5; Psalm 2:4; James 1:2–4; 1 Peter 5:6–10

Aim: TO LEARN THAT when the troubled times are over, God's children "come forth as pure gold." TO BE MINDFUL OF THE FACT THAT troubled times often teach you how to lean on the Lord in a way that you never have before. TO REALIZE THAT we are helped in the process of troubled times in our lives and don't even know it sometimes until much later.

Song: God Will Provide; The Lord Will Make a Way

Did you ever stop to think about the lovingkindness of God? If you did, you would discover that it knows no bounds. You would discover that it is strong in that it chastises, protects, trains (prepares), and cares. You would discover that it employs tough love to rid us of some undesirable habits while molding us and instilling lacking habits and attributes within us.

If I had never suffered any trouble, then there would be no way that the remembrance of my trouble and how bereft I felt before the Lord rescued me could benefit you in your troubled times because I would not have that memory to draw upon. But as I told you in Lesson 2, I remember how it felt when trouble hit my life, how it felt during my rainy season, and how it felt when the storm was over. And that is something I tell everywhere I go. And that is why I can tell you with assurance that, if you are troubled, help is on the way if you are God's child, so keep your faith.

Why
Understanding the "Why" of things
Can make for easier acceptance of
Some of the changes that life brings.
However, it is not given to us to understand
Everything that comes to hand because if that
Happened, we would no longer be walking by faith
But by everything that happened in accordance
With the way we had our lives planned.
Having faith in Him is a necessary requirement
Of making it to that other land
And since I know that He already has a life plan
For me anyway, I will just lean on Him and
Trust Him to take care of me no matter what
Happens because the stories in the Bible,
Things taught me by my Mother and
Things that have occurred in my
Life, reassure me that He can.

****

BIBLE EXAMPLES

Oo–wee! Glad That's Not Me

The first Bible example I want to talk about is Joseph, owner of the coat of many colors. You know Joseph was much loved by his daddy, Jacob, right? Yes, he was loved so much that his daddy had him a coat of many colors made. Nice gesture, don't you think? Uhm–hmm. Well, y'all know the story, so I won't prolong it. (Genesis 37, 39, 40 & 41)

But I will tell you that Joseph has a special place in my life and always has. Why? Well, I can identify with him. He had dreams at night as a child, and so did I. He was the victim of jealousy, and so was I and some of it still exists to this day. (The names and faces have changed over the years, but the problem of jealousy still exists. But that's all right because I know God has plans for me. {Romans 8:31} A good piece to read concerning jealousy is *Chopping My Row*, Lesson 9.)

At any rate, that boy's brothers were so jealous of him that they planned to kill him. But it didn't happen like that because God had plans for him. He was sold into slavery, but that was God's plan all along. I remember being oh so sorry that happened to Joseph. But so, so glad that it was not me.

I was so glad to have a Momma who loved me that I sometimes would run inside from playing to tell her I was glad she was my Momma. Of course, she looked taken aback, but I found out later that she puzzled over things I said and did quite a bit.

Moving back to Joseph, remember how he had dreamed of life down in Egypt before it ever happened. Yes, folks, I was like Joseph in that I dreamed things happening before they did, too. How? Why? I told y'all, my Momma often told me that something had been trying to get my attention all my life. I don't understand it, and that's okay. I just accept the fact that I am a bit strange. That is why I am driven to write for you. There is something on the inside that is like fire, and it is lessened when I encourage you by my writing about the goodness of God.

Joseph was thrown into prison unjustly. But that worked out as well. God used some of the dreams he interpreted while in prison to get him out. Never forget how he got the ability to dream of the future in the first place. God was in the plan, and He made Joseph rise to the top.

He Didn't Bother Anybody

Now let's take a look at Daniel, the three Hebrew boys, David, and Moses.

I have a lesson I sometimes do for ladies' days that is entitled, "If the Lord…" I take those last few words of the preceding sentence from the Scripture Romans 8:31 which says, "If the Lord is for us, who can be against us?" and I break it down. I paraphrased that Scripture a bit, but you get my drift. We will come back to that statement toward the end of the lesson, so stick a pin in it.

But first I want to ask you something. Why do you suppose we have trouble? I figure like this:

Christians have trouble because they have given their allegiance to God. And you know the Scripture says all who live Godly shall suffer persecution. (Timothy 3:12, KJV)

Why was Daniel thrown into the lions' den? We know that God was working behind the scenes because He had already talked to the lions and made sure they knew what was what. Either that or He locked the lions' jaws and crippled their claws or immobilized them. Though the lions did not eat Daniel, we do know that the lions were hungry because of the fate of the men who were thrown in later.

Get Yourself Up

Why were the three Hebrew boys thrown into the fiery furnace? He was working behind the scenes because He was already in the fire waiting for them and suffered them to come to no harm.

Why did David have to hide from Saul? Working behind the scenes when He had Jonathan, Saul's son, to tell David to flee because it was not safe for him any longer at Saul's place.

Why did Pharaoh tell Moses to see his face no more because on the day he did, Pharaoh would have him killed? Working behind the scenes because He had already said He would show His powers in Egypt. Had already arranged for the angel to go to the homes that did not have the blood on the doorposts.

I could give many other examples, but the ones listed above are enough for our lesson today. Here's the thing. All the people mentioned above were in trouble because they all were trying to carry out the will of God.

So, that ought to tell you that if you are trying to carry out God's will for your life, you will suffer for it.

Why didn't they stop when they were threatened with death? What drove them to keep going despite mortal peril? Why would God let them go through so much when all they were trying to do was serve Him?

Oh, but wait a minute! We can see from the people above that, though they had some hard knocks and some trials while trying to do their work for the Lord, God had them in mind all the time. He had a plan and was working on it all the while, sort of like behind the scenes (more about this later in the lesson).

Now you know why it is necessary to have faith and how it can make you feel like a million even though the weight of the world is resting on your shoulders. I told you earlier that 1 Peter 1:5–7 says God cares for you.

Boxed-in Canyon Times (Rainy Seasons)

Now, let's talk about some of the times in our lives that make us question the "why" of things or about times in our lives when we have been running from our enemies and have run until we are in a boxed-in canyon. And you can hear your enemy exclaim with glee, "Aw–w, we got her now!"

Those words have been uttered many times in the life of a child of God, but you know what? The foe, the enemy or whatever title or name they go by, forgot that the Shepherd is always mindful of His sheep. I'm so glad I am one of His sheep because all I have to do is open my feeble mouth and say, "Father it's me. I'm in trouble and I wonder do You see what they are trying to do to me? I don't mean to be a bother and I don't mean to be a pain, but I need to come in out of this storm and the rain. Can You hear me? Did You hear the glee in my enemy's words when they said, 'We got her now. The God that she serves must be asleep or He might be dead. At any rate, it doesn't matter; He ain't looking now. This is the chance <u>we</u> have been waiting and hoping for!'"

I underlined the word "we" in the sentence above because that is often the way God's children enemies come at them. If you look in the annals of Biblical history, you will see this. But I don't understand why and how the enemies of God's children think they can get past His ever–watchful eyes. *(Psalm 94:7–9, KJV)*

Sometimes I want to say, "Don't you know that no weapon

formed against me shall be victorious? Even if, for whatever reason, He leaves me alone for a while, don't you know that He will, if I bleat; He will, if I cry; He will, if I whimper; He will, come to see about me? And He will bring His rod, His staff and whatever weapon from His arsenal that is needed? Don't be so jubilant and joyful that you have me on the run and have me boxed in because, don't you know that while I was running, I was bleating; while I was running, I was whimpering; while I was running, I was crying in prayer to my Father, I AM? All I can say to you is that I wouldn't want to be you."

I have seen God take my enemies and change circumstances in their lives so that they had to come to me, needing a big favor that only I could grant. And I did it without malice, and you know why? I do not want to have to learn a particular lesson again, so I try to do what I should. I mean life is hard enough as it is. I'm not about to knowingly add to my duress.

The details of these scenarios would make for some interesting reading, let me tell you! But some things you keep in your heart, with an attitude of gratitude, and puzzle over them or marvel at your being saved.

So, reader, for the times that you may be boxed in by your enemies or life's circumstances, keep a close relationship with God so that He will hear your bleating, your whimpering, and your crying. For He will make everything all right. And whatever you do, never underestimate the prayers of the saints that we mentioned in Lesson 2.

<u>Case in Point</u> – Another House Fire Lesson

You already know from the previous lessons that I suffered a house fire back in 1987. I told you how people of all races came to my aid. That made my mouth fall open and put a smile on my face. (In my mind, I remember thinking that the way people were acting was the caring way that God wanted us to act all the time! Yes, I was amazed. I did not know it then but have since learned and teach it each time I talk about my house fire, that there are blessings and lessons in all troubles that happen in our lives. Here again, I reference my book *Chopping My Row*, Lessons 2 and 3.)

Allow me to take the time and walk you through the gamut of emotions I felt during the time of my fire.

When I received the summons to our school office to tell me my house was burning down, I was stunned. As a matter of fact, when the school secretary told me, one of my aides was standing there with me, so naturally, I assumed the secretary was talking to her. I mean, stuff like that, just didn't happen to me.

So I turned to the aide, who had grabbed her chest and had thrown herself against the wall in what was going to be histrionics of the first order. But the school secretary quickly told the aide, "Not your house, but yours." And she was pointing at me! I was incredulous and I remember saying in a questioning tone, "MY house is burning down?!" The secretary said, "Yes, we just got the call."

Y'all, I was so flummoxed I could barely think. Then I thought, *I guess I need to go home.* My aide and another special education aide, who is a member of the church, (white congregation - will explain the mention of race in a little bit) decided to go along with me to my house. The aide said, "Alma, you give me those keys. You don't need to be driving right now." And I, like a shell–shocked lamb, handed them over to her.

Get Yourself Up

Our house at the time, was in a town about five miles from the town where I taught school and about three miles out in the country from there. That meant we had to travel about eight miles to get to my house. Since this was in a rural area, we could see a tall column of billowing smoke with flames in it as we drove along the highway. One person said, that is not your house, Alma, because it is too far away. The other aide said, I'm glad it is not her house because that is a hot fire. You can see the flames billowing up in it.

We drove on to the next town and turned to take the rural route that led to my house. It was a curving and winding road, but we all three concluded that it must be my house because every time we went around a curve that took us away from the billowing column of fire and smoke, the next curve took us back toward it. And sure enough it was!

The take charge aide said to me, "Alma, when you get to that house, don't you go in!"

I said with a deadly conviction in my voice, "Then I'd better see my Momma when I get to that house."

And when we got there, I saw lots of people milling, standing around agog, but I saw my Momma standing looking shocked over in a bean field. I ran up to her and hugged her and pulled the burnt end of her plait off her head. She was fine. Then I turned my attention to the house.

Well, correct that. It was a two-house fire. My mother's house which was across the driveway from mine was already burned completely down and mine was half gone. I stood there as the wind gently rippled the tiny bean sprouts in the field, and watched my living room, my son's room and my bedroom go up in flames and there was not a thing I could do about it.

I remember wondering why the wind was gently blowing the bean sprouts in the field as if nothing was wrong. Didn't the world know, "MY HOUSE WAS BURNING DOWN!" I remember looking at the fire and thinking that everything that I had worked toward for 13 years was going up in smoke. I was so mad at the Lord. I looked up at the sky and thought about raising my fist to the sky and asking Him if He hadn't already done enough to me. Humph, just as quickly as that thought came, came a rational one said, "This is God you are talking about," and with that rational thought, I dropped my head and cast my eyes to the ground and the tears started rolling. Somebody came up and said, "You had insurance, right?"

That's when it hit me that, nope, we did not, because he had changed the policy and there was a one-week lapse in coverage between when the grace period ended and the new one took effect. Yep, you guessed it. My house fire occurred during the one week there was no coverage at all! Yep, surely did!

Somebody suggested calling my husband who worked at Goodyear and they went to their house to call him. There were no fire trucks there for the longest because we did not have rural fire protection, either. Finally, the town that was three miles away sent a pumper, but there was no source of water once they had used the water that they had on the truck. The firemen were pulling their hair, but it did not do Alma's house any good. It was blazing fast! Goody too–shoes Alma's house was burning down to the ground!

So, I was filled with bitterness because I kept telling myself,

Get Yourself Up

"That's what you get for always trying to treat everybody right! That's what you **get**!"

I remember people kept telling me, "These things can be replaced." I remembered how hard it had been to get those *things* in the first place and I knew it was not going to be easy. I was back at square one! So full was my venom that I thought to myself that the next person who says, "These things can be replaced," is going to get a blasting from me.

And sure enough, the take charge aide said it. I quipped out, "You just tell me how?" She did not answer, and I said, "That's what I thought! You are going home to your house intact tonight while I do not even own a broom straw! So, don't even tell me about stuff being replaced. I do not want to hear it!" She never said a word.

So, after my husband had arrived and the fire was out, we left. The take charge aide was still driving my vehicle and I knew we were on our way to school where they had left their cars. I had made plans to meet my husband at his aunt's house where my children were and that is what my mind was on, getting to them and breaking the news to them. My husband's aunt or uncle one, had picked them up from school, but had not told them anything.

As I said, my mind was on getting to my babies! So, I was very irritated when one of the aides (the take charge one) said she had to stop by her house before I dropped them off at school. She saw I was irritated and said it would be quick! I had already been so mean to her, I just figured that she didn't know how I was feeling or just didn't care. I could not WAIT to get her out of my car and my attitude showed that, too!

And when the aide who had to run into her house for a few minutes came out, my mouth fell open. She had armloads of clothing for my son! She went back in and came out with several pairs of shoes, sweaters, and what–have–you. She had just outfitted my son for the rest of the school term and for the summer. I remember thinking that the Lord was providing for me because He knew I could hardly formulate a thought without tears welling up in my eyes.

When I looked at the aide, I apologized for speaking to her like I had earlier, to which she replied, "Don't worry about it. I understand. You are holding up a lot better than I would have. In fact, I would have thought something was wrong with you if you had not responded as you did, especially about the baby pictures."

I cried some more, but not for long because I had a warm glow on the inside because I knew that my Father was opening hearts and doors for me.

She had just given me what, years later, I would call *a care package* from the Lord, and it was tailor–made with my name on it. That lesson told me God had been working behind the scenes all the time. But I did not give it that terminology at the time. That would come to me years on down the road.

I won't go into all the details, but I wanted to let you know that another lesson I learned from my house fire is that material things come and go and are not what life is all about. They are just things to hurt if you get too attached to them. Now, I use the things I own and am appreciative of them, but I know that is where it stops.

Whatever God blesses me with, I will be thankful for, but things will never occupy the place in life that they used to. I mean, before the fire, I had things I planned for my children to have as heirlooms, etc.

Now, I know what real life is about and that is loving God and loving my fellowman as myself. That's the real deal.

Still, I mean, I didn't think I was overly materialistic, because I gave several people who were down on themselves expensive rings of mine and watches and even bought watches and rings for some of my disadvantaged students to build their self-esteem.

You see, because I knew what it felt like to be from a poor home, I helped my children in ways I knew would be something special to them. I mean, I remember how I felt as a child when other girls in my class had beautiful birthstone rings that were real gold and would not turn your finger green. And I remember how I longed for one.

I knew how I felt after I got grown if I got a beautiful ring. So, I was passing the favor along, making them feel good while they waited to grow up in life. I'm saying all that to say I guess I thought my caring deeds were insurance against bad stuff happening. I was naive, but I have learned, in that, I know that everything happens for a reason and that if you live for the Lord, you will suffer persecution in some form or another. But experience, and the Word, have also taught me that joy comes in the morning.

Case in Point – My Rock, My Go to Person

I mentioned in Lesson Three about my strong tower, as far as humans go. As I said, that had always been my Momma. But there comes a time in all our lives that there is a shift in our norm. The boundaries of the world as we have known it change, and we know things can never be the same. The only thing that we know is that we have the same name, but that the person we were has been forever changed, sometimes to the extent that we no longer know who we really are. That is the type of shift that changes you so that you realize life is not all about you anymore. That is what began to happen to me when I lost my Momma.

I told you back in Lesson 2 that Momma has always been my strong tower, my go-to person. Let me tell you a bit of history about my relationship with her. I was the only girl in my family out of three children. My Momma and Daddy separated when I was just past the toddler stage, so all I knew was my Momma and her fierce love for me. So, when she became sick, the wheels on my train came to a screeching halt until I learned how to deal with the new change and started my motor back up and kept smoothly running on.

Every now and again, her sickness would rattle her body and shake my foundation, and at such times my train would almost wobble and almost stop. But I would make the necessary changes while keeping an even closer vigil on Momma.

But one day, Lord help me, my Momma left me in this world by myself. My world was not right anymore. She had always been there for me to talk things over with, etc. My train came to a screeching halt, and nothing and nobody could say the right things to make it any better! My Momma was gone, the foundation that had been my constant, gone! I did not have time for drama or foolishness of any type. If you crossed me at that time, I told you about yourself and moved on.

That was during the first month of my grief. I felt like here I was trying to figure out the mess that my life was, and some drama queen or king was ranting about something that did not amount to a hill of beans. During that time, the usually docile me would tell a person with terse words, "Get over it already!" And they usually left me alone or looked at me and asked, "Are you okay?"

To which I might respond, "As okay as is possible!" or "Whatever!"

That was the grief speaking and me trying to find myself since there was a great big gaping hole in the tracks that my train used to run on. My grief had me boxed in.

But you know what? When such a shift in our norm, as mentioned above, takes place, that is the time to lean on God. During shifts in our norm, we usually learn the meaning of, "Let go and let God," if we don't already know the meaning of those words. And sometimes, even if we do know the meaning, we find there is a depth of leaning that exists that we did not know until said shift happened in our lives.

Not all shifts in the norm are negative, though they may enter the scene seemingly that way. What happened to me was as natural as the rain that washes the earth. I knew that already, but that did not make the shift in my norm any less painful.

So, when I thought about my Momma and the things she had been teaching me my whole life, I reached for them. I reached for my God in a way that I never had before, and that is saying a lot because I already had an intimate relationship with Him. My soul took over my prayers and spoke to Him on my behalf because I just could not do it, y'all.

My train track was being repaired with prayers that could not be uttered. The Holy Spirit spoke from my soul to my God. I remember asking the Lord to make the pain go away and telling Him that I knew she had to go, but that it hurt so much. I told Him I could accept it if He would just make the pain go away–y–y. That big ache which made it so that I could not eat left me, and then my appetite came back, and I could do more than drink water and sip Mountain Dew. I began to nibble here and there.

———————————

You know, I remember Momma told me about two weeks before she died that I would become a very successful author. At the time, writing anything was just a far thought back in my mind because I was still teaching. It was all I could do to get through the teaching day, get home to prepare the evening meal and get her supper over to her and visit with her a bit.

But dealing with my kids at school and my teaching responsibilities made my loss bearable when she passed two weeks later. In the long hours between work and the beginning of the next school day was where I had the most difficult time.

With my hand in His hand like the toddler I used to be when my Momma held my hand, I began to take my first sure enough steps alone, but not alone. I was buoyed up by my best Friend, God. I have weathered many storms since then and have come to realize that my life is not all about me, now, but about pleasing the God of Heaven.

Through the teaching and learning and growing process, after I lost my Momma, I realized that God had me in His arms and had me all the time. I realized that He rocked me when I needed it and sent tender angels of thought and comfort to me as I began my new run on my repaired tracks. I did not run with the speed I used to at first but with a deeper purpose and meaning.

Getting Re–equipped for the Lord's Work

This is the way I had life figured before this particular earth–shattering week. I figured that since I had to put my Momma in the ground all those years ago and had made it through that, then I could handle most anything. Ha! Ha! Ha! Ha! That is almost laughable!

Then came the time that was worse than the time I thought was my worst. For the past week, I have been living in a rainy season. I have been existing in a vacuum. I didn't stop blogging daily because I knew there are some of you who depend on reading my blog and others who, though you might not depend on it, do like to read it. So what I did was reach within a ready-made source and keep the blog going with minimal effort, while I got the furnace of my faith restoked.

Yes, you guessed it; I reached for my book, *W.O.W. Created w.o.w.* as the source of easy inspirational pieces. You see, I figured that since I knew the book inside and out, since I was its author, I wouldn't have to think very much at all as I worked my way through my painful situation.

What I had not counted on was being fed poems and information to include in the blog and feeding myself in the process! The book that God gave me the inspiration to write was now feeding me, as well as others! The daily doing of the blog pushed the shards of my faith back together and the telephone call that I received, from a friend whose husband was terminally ill, cemented it back together for me. She thanked me profusely for the writing of the book and told me she carried it everywhere she went, hospital and all.

W.O.W.! Talk about being rejuvenated! Umph, umph, umph! What a mighty God we serve! I am reminded of Maya Angelou's words to "be a rainbow in somebody else's cloud." (On YouTube, *Dr. Maya Angelou: Be A Rainbow in Somebody Else's Cloud*, | Oprah's Masterclass, May 28, 2014, https://youtu.be/0nYXFletWH4)

Struggling Under a Heavy Load

Have you ever met Coincidence along your journey in life? And the meeting was so smooth as to join with your life without a single hitch. Such a meeting often does not come with fanfare, you just look up, and He is there. At any rate, as I walk this Christian journey, more and more I realize that to Jesus we are precious. We are God's children, and as such, we are somebody. It does not matter what the world may say, to Jesus we are somebody, and that is all we need.

This story poem was placed on my heart this morning. I hope it speaks to your soul in a positive way:

You Are Somebody
If fame or fortune is never reached
Be able to say that you helped somebody
By the actions that your life preached.
Every kind word and every kind deed
Is noted by Heavenly recorders against the time
In your life that you may find yourself in need.

Get Yourself Up

You know, if I walk this world and have a care
About the problems you face and the burdens you bear
Jesus sees my loving concern and
Loves and cherishes me in return.
If I come upon you struggling with a heavy load
As you walk along life's ever winding road
And use my shoulders to help lighten your pack
By shifting some of the load onto my own back,
Jesus takes note of what I have done
And marks me as a loving and faithful one.
And if while walking with our shared load
We begin a dialogue about my just happening along
Just when you had begun to despair
Because of the heavy burden that you had to bear
And in that discussion, you hear me voice
A long–held belief that because we are
Special to Jesus, He makes life paths intertwine in such a way
That they touch at crucial points and times during our stay.
That sets you to thinking and thinking about coincidence
And you take from the conversation a newfound belief
That because you are precious to Him
God will always send you effective relief.
You feel so much better that you break out in song.
And I join you as we raise our voices together
To share with all passersby our "faithful God" song.
We sing, laugh, and talk for a good long while
And when our paths diverge, we part with a smile
You with your burden fully reloaded on your back
But with renewed vigor, confidence, and a newfound realization
That the pack on your back, though it is the same
Seems so much lighter than before I came.
In puzzlement, you take a quick look back
At the stranger who helped you so

And to your astonishment, you wonder aloud
"Hey, where did he go?"
You continue your journey with my words ringing in your ears
"You must be somebody special for the Lord
To change my schedule just to bolster you up
and allay your fears."
You find that there is a new spring in your step
And a soothing but peppy melody in your brain
That repeats itself over and over in a constant
but pleasant refrain.
"I'm somebody in Jesus; I don't walk alone "no mo."
I'm somebody in Jesus, and I can tell this load on my back
"You ain't nothing but a means that Jesus
used to rebuild my faith
And with but a few short strides I will lay you down
Though, I will always carry with me the day that Coincidence
Visited me and left me with a faith more profound.
Thank You, Coincidence, for your teaching visit with me
'Cause now I know that God will carry me
From point A to point Z
Because, in Jesus, I am somebody!"

****

There is a song on YouTube entitled, "Somebody in Jesus" by the Southside Singers I wish you would go and listen to. It will bless your spirit as it does mine each time I hear it. And remember, Jesus loves you so the darts of the world, though at times hurtful, can do no lasting damage.

Broken and Fixed

I was in Dollar Tree last night and there was a lady and two kids behind me in the LONG line. One was a big kid, one a toddler. The bigger one had a pack of glow sticks and the baby was screaming for them, so the Mom opened the pack and gave him one, which stopped the tears. He walked around with it smiling, but then the bigger boy took it and the baby started screaming again. Just as the Mom was about to fuss at the older child, he bent the glow stick and handed it back to the baby. As we walked outside at the same time, the baby noticed the stick was now glowing and his brother said, "I had to break it so you could get the full effect from it."

Sometimes in life, we must be broken just like the glow stick so we can fulfill the purpose for which we were created. Just like the baby was contented to just walk around swinging the unbroken glow stick because he didn't know what it was created to do, we often are content with just "being" because we don't understand what we were created to do. Sometimes our being broken means we have to get sick, go through a divorce, experience the sickness or death of a spouse, loved ones, parents, best friends, etc. But oftentimes, it is in those moments of desperation, when we are broken that we then we can see why we were created – to glow.

The Beat Goes On

It is true that we will be learning as long as we live, but that is a fact we sometimes forget.

The same is true of living a Christian life. While we are living, our learning continues, as does the Lord's love for us.

Sometimes we must learn painful lessons in life, like the lesson the baby learned with the glow stick.

But you know what I have discovered? I have found that when a Christian goes through a tough lesson, the love of God is with Him. You see, whatever you go through in life, The Lord God is aware of it, and as a matter of fact, was aware of it before it happened. We are still wrapped in His loving arms. Even when we are being taught some tough lessons. You know the Bible says the "Lord chastises those that He loves." (Hebrews 12:6–7, 11 KJV) So go ahead and learn your lesson and learn it well so that it does not have to be repeated. Remember the "Lord God deals with us as with sons." (Proverbs 3:12; Hebrews 12:6)

Learn your lessons as you lean on His love, ever secure in the knowledge that He cares for you.

Case in Point – Lessons from My Life

My Attention
As I have looked within and back and have indeed seen that the benevolent God I serve is working behind the scenes all the time. I have found throughout my life that God has been mindful of me and has been moving mountains for my good.

You, dear one, carry the love of Jesus deep in your heart and every now and then, He allows you to be reminded of that fact by the coincidences that occur in your life, such as your deciding, of all days, to read this book today or be in this class today.

Whoever you are, precious one, know that Jesus loves you so. How can I say that? Easily, He had me to take an ordinary part of life in this world and break it down into a story poem ("You Are Somebody") in such a manner that it has you wondering, "Is she talking to me? Nah, just coincidence."

Do you really think so? I can tell you this, there is no such thing as coincidence in life! You were meant to read the portion of the book we covered including my story poem, so let it reassure you and bless you. And remember like I always say, "God sees, He knows, and He cares!" How wonderful it is to be somebody in Jesus because you are wrapped up in His love!

But you know, even today, people make the mistake of thinking that the Shepherd, Jesus, no longer cares for or guards the sheep. They fail to bear in mind that the Lord God told us that He is faithful and, as such, is ever tending and getting the sheep safely home to the place He has prepared for them.

Don't you fear little sheep because your enemies have caused God in Heaven to laugh. (Psalms 2:4)

When the Fire Doesn't Burn

I want to elaborate a bit more about times like the ones mentioned above, I call these, *"times when the fire doesn't burn."* I am speaking of those occasions in your life when your ship was on its way to sinking, and you had no way of extricating yourself from the situation; those times when all your hope was gone because your enemies had done their best to inflict their worst on you and had moved on to torture someone else because they knew you were done. You know the times in your life when you wanted to despair but had been in a particular rainy season for so long you became resigned to "The enemy would win or that they had finally gotten you." And you had resigned yourself to the fact *that this was the way it was going to be*, so, it had to be God's will. You do know the kinds of times I am talking about, right? As I said earlier, those boxed in times.

Well, remember that just when you had become resigned to the direness of a given situation and just as you were thinking it was time to get ready for packing it all in concerning that situation, an unflappable feeling of peace stole into your being and you, with wonder, realized that everything was going to be all right? You felt so relieved that you wanted to skip or maybe you wanted to go through the rest of the day with your arms wound tightly around yourself secure in the secret knowledge of that assurance.

Folks, when you are in *"times when the fire doesn't burn,"* know assuredly that the Shepherd, Who has been watching your situation all along, is showing your enemies that you are His, and as such, not to trifle with you. I like to think that the Shepherd is in the laughing mode (Psalm 2:4) during these times. In other words, your enemies are getting ready to be chopped liver in that, the plan that they had for you, or worse, has become their own. I'm talking about the times when you feel yourself wrapped in God's love, when inexplicable peace comes to you, and you see the situation(s) that you thought was impossible to get out of, being unwound and fixed and the pain of that situation going away. Y'all know the times I am talking about, the times the Bible calls, "Peace that surpasseth all understanding," Those are the times when you can see the ministration of the God of Heaven in your life doing His "love thing" or "love stuff." (Philippians 4:7–9, NKJV)

And if your enemies were wise, they would beg you to forgive them and pray for them, but as so often is the case, enemies get so caught up in being victorious over you, that they fail to realize that except it be God's will for a season, they will never best you because you are God's child. This is the time of your deliverance and the time that your enemy finally recognizes he is fighting a Force so much bigger than you. This is the time your enemy realizes that he is contending with God Almighty.

Let me suggest something to you. I don't have to suggest you savor the moment of your deliverance because you are going to do that anyway. But while you are savoring the moment, savor it to the extent that you can call that moment back up to your fellowman who may be going through something similar and needing assurance; savor it to the point that you use it to step higher for the God of Heaven, Who has done marvelous things in your life. If you do that, my friend, you will be doing well and making our Father smile as He has these things recorded in your portion of the Book of Life.

> He was thrown into the fire because
> His enemies wanted to see him squirm
> But they were dismayed to discover
> That their fire did not even burn.

Yes, my precious, if you but take the time and look back over your life, you will realize that you, too, have been through some times when *the fire did not even burn*, though you did not know it at the time.

The Next Time

So, the **next time** you are under assault by whomever or whatever, just wait for your change. Call up in your mind the time of your last rescue that I asked you to savor and rest in assurance of the fact that your Father is still working behind the scenes in your life to orchestrate things according to His purpose.

Woo! Just think, little sheep, the Creator, Himself is moving on your behalf! When the trouble has been eradicated, if you have been faithful in your adherence to Him, God will get the glory and your enemies will become wary of you, frightened, even, to bother you, or more determined. But by the time word gets around, most folks will not willingly trouble you and those who do will find out the same thing Pharaoh learned too late in His life, that it does not pay to trifle with the people of God. They will finally learn that God is not always going to be longsuffering when it comes to His children's cries. They will learn that when He decides to move, He gives no quarter. It will be too late to say, "Uh, oops, I'm sorry."

How can I say this? Easily, because I can hear the tumult of the chariot wheels coming off as the "Egyptians tried to turn and retreat from Israel when they said, 'Let us run because the Lord is fighting for them.'" (Exodus 14:25, KJV) But it did them no good. There was to be no escape that day; they ended up lying in a watery grave!

Against the Day of Trouble

Read the Scripture, Job 38:22. The Scripture talks about the storehouses of the Lord that He has in waiting for the day of trouble. When I read about the storehouses of the Lord, I thought about Him doing battle with Pharaoh and some of the other enemies of God's people, Israel.

And I remember how the word went around to the other enemies of God's people and the enemies were afraid to bother them. *(2 Chronicles 20:29)*

Moving forward to today, I know whatever comes up against His people, the Lord is prepared. And when I remember the storehouses, I get gladdened within my spirit.

So–o, I have determined that when my enemy seems to get the best of me, it is only because there is a lesson in it for me. Then I think like the Hebrew boys, "If the Lord doesn't deliver me, it's not because He can't." I remember the storehouses my Father has, and I step on. You see, I know that my redeemer liveth and that He cares for me. 1 Peter 3:12 & Job 19:25.

When the time comes that your world falls apart, don't be so miserable that you cause everyone around you to be miserable; so miserable that your enemies get to laugh and say, "See, I told you she/he was not all they were purported to be!" Don't give God's enemies something to crow about. Just remember God's storehouses and wait for your change to come.

Being Tried by the Fire

If in the coming year, you encounter some situations that fairly knock you to your knees, I hope you remember to read, James 1:2–4, NASB.

Verse 2 – Consider it all joy, my brethren, when you encounter various trials.

Verse 3 – Knowing that the testing of your faith produces endurance.

Verse 4 – And let endurance have its perfect result, that you may be perfect and complete, lacking nothing. (PURE GOLD?)
The passage of Scripture quoted on the previous page is a good tool to have in your bag or satchel of preparations for a spiritual rebirth or drawing closer to God.

Savor the Victory

When the next skirmish hits your life savor the victory of your last one and keep trusting God. For sure, there will be other instances in your life that you do not understand but it doesn't matter now. You don't have to understand why things happen as they do; that is not a prerequisite of pleasing God, but having faith is. So, if you have the wisdom to trust the Good Lord, then you will believe and know that no matter what comes up in your life, He will be there just like He was the last time. And that is a powerful thing to come to know. That wisdom will carry you on when it seems you should be beaten down and done. That belief will keep you struggling and striving to reach its Source, Jehovah, God.

Stay the course whatever you do and remember the more adverse your situation, the bigger blessing you will receive if you just remain faithful to God. Somebody just thought, "Say what?! Say again." And I will repeat the gist of what I said. The tougher the trials(s) you go through, the bigger blessing you will have if you remain faithful, the whole way through.

Remember Job. (Job Chapters, 1, 2 & 42, KJV) Remain faithful when you don't understand, and when it seems the whole world is conspiring against you to such a degree that you cannot smile, smile anyway. There is no problem you have that the Lord is not aware of, but you keep praying and keep stepping on.

And one day you will find that you have stepped from the craggy rocks you had been climbing to smooth and cooling stairs of marble and from there to a moving stairway as you make your miraculous climb to the top.

Get Yourself Up

You will find that just like you could not seem to catch a break for anything, the breaks will fall into your lap at every turn. You will be overwhelmed with gratitude, and you will turn to the God of Heaven and thank Him for working for you all the time and for opening your insight further so you could recognize that fact. And then you will be like an announcer with a mega horn or a news commentator with a new piece of broadcasting equipment in that you will shout the goodness of God from the tallest mountain in your world. You will tell everybody, and you will not be ashamed to do it. In fact, you will talk so much about it that folk might not want to listen. But that's okay, keep an upbeat outlook on life and be ready to tell all who ask about the goodness and faithfulness of the God you serve anyway.

He commands the sea, wind, water, blacksmiths' coals, in fact, all creation. Who better to take with you the rest of your life than God Himself? If you believe in Him strongly enough, I think He knows it and is pleased by it and walks with you. Therefore, I believe He makes "All things work together for your good." (Romans 8:28, KJV) When He gets finished with you, you shall come forth as pure gold. (Job 23:10, KJV)

We talked earlier about being tried by the fire so here is a poem to speak to the fire that tried to destroy your life but only served to build your hope. While this poem speaks to a literal fire it speaks of so much more, God's faithful, teaching, pruning and molding love! **(PURE GOLD?)**

Fire, Fire, Fire, Fire
Fire, fire, fire, fire
You tried hard to make me lose
The dreams to which I aspire.
You made me weep like a baby

Upon the loss of the material things
That working for thirteen years had
Allowed me to gain
But you still will not wreck my world again
Because I have learned a lesson that is good
From the ashes that you allowed to remain.
"Material things count for nothing, mortal man
It is the spiritual things that matter and
Putting your trust in the Lord, Who
Can save your soul, and only He can."
Fire, fire, fire, fire
I still have dreams to which I aspire
But they cannot be touched by the likes of you
Because they are built around my Father
Who has taught me to know what I should value.

Recognize Who He Is

When you have been delivered enough times and been in rainy seasons and fiery trials often enough, you will start to shine as pure gold.

Why is Faith Priceless?

Feb, 13, 22

Have you ever had a time when you wanted to despair, but because of your belief that God would, somehow, make everything all right, you didn't? Then you have come to understand how faith is priceless.

- That statement means you can go to sleep at night when your world has been turned upside down. (Philippians 4:7, NKJV)
- It means you don't have to wring your hands in

despair because you think all hope is gone and there is nothing you can do about it.

- It means that folk will look at you and marvel at how you can still smile in the face of adversity.

Yes, my friend, it means you have been running your race for the Lord long enough to know that He begins where our possible ends. And you know that all things are possible with Him. And remember, He does His best when we are tapped out.

I will tell you what I mean by tapped out in a few seconds, but first I want to share with you what I put on my Twitter account recently. I put these words: "God said to trust Him, and I will because this will not be the first mountain that faith has moved." By the preceding statement, I mean there is a situation that seems to be impossible to work out. The impossible situation could be anything that a person has worked on and worked on until there is nothing else to try. The person could have exhausted every avenue and knows there is nothing else to be done about it. The previous sentence tells us what *tapped out* means, *done all you could do, tried every way possible and know without a doubt that, "That's just the way it is."*

"That's just the way it is." I heard those words often as a child, but I never gave up on something I really wanted without asking the Lord about it. I never told my Momma that I had prayed about an impossible situation, but I often did. I prayed and then I waited on the Lord. If the situation worked out, and it did often enough, I knew that the Lord had answered, "Yes." If the situation did not work out, I knew that the answer was, "No or not right now." I had enough seemingly impossible situations to be worked out so that my faith and trust in God grew by leaps and bounds.

Hold On to Your Faith at All Costs! It Is Priceless!

Our minds are not the minds of God. His ways are higher than ours as are His thoughts. I used to wonder why certain things happened to me until I read the 38th chapter of the book of Job. I don't wonder anymore. I just trust in Him and keep that green statement from Lesson 2 among the uppermost thoughts in my mind, and I keep stepping.

You see, I don't understand how and why a bridge holds me, but I trust it to do so. And never let it be said that I have more faith in a bridge than I do the God of Heaven. I have learned to trust Him in all things and to know there is a reason for everything that happens in my life, be it good or be it bad. I enjoy the good and thank Him for it. I ask His help in making it through the bad while praising Him and thanking Him for the good that is in my life and for my ultimate deliverance by a faithful God. And then what do I do? Yep, you got it. I keep stepping because I have seen my God show me many times, "I got this!"

I Got This, Part 2

I am going to talk a little about four Scriptures, Isaiah 41:10–13; Isaiah 43:1–2; Psalm 23; and Psalm 46. While there are a plethora of Scriptures that I could use, these four will do for our purposes.

There have been so many times I found myself in a particular situation and could find nowhere, no man–made place to turn. But I had a Father Who sits high and looks low. He sees everything that goes on because He made the eyes. He hears everything that goes on because He made the ears. And He has stepped in right on time for me on numerous occasions.

Case in Point

As a teacher, it was nothing for me to hear my students use the phrase, "I got this!" The utterance of that phrase meant that whoever uttered it was most certain they could handle with ease a particular task that others perceived as having an insurmountable degree of difficulty. And more often than not, they would handle it with finesse.

Now, I like to imagine that God handles the trivial little things we lay at His feet in the same manner. For, I know there is nothing too hard for Him. (Genesis 18:14) And I do mean nothing.

****

There are four more Scriptures I want to discuss with you about the Lord God's assurance of His love and care. You remember that I told you that, "The things that were written before times were written for our learning." (Romans 15:4, KJV)

So, let's learn a new or renewed lesson from this Scripture: "Fear not, for I am with you; be not dismayed, for I am your God; I will strengthen you, I will help you, I will uphold you with my righteous right hand. Behold, all who are incensed against you shall be put to shame and confounded; those who strive against you shall be as nothing and shall perish. You shall seek those who contend with you, but you shall not find them; those who war against you shall be as nothing at all. For I, the Lord your God, hold your right hand; it is I who say to you, "Fear not, I am the One who helps you." (Isaiah 41:10–13, KJV)

That is a powerful passage of Scripture full of assurance. It says, and I will paraphrase: Are you worried? Don't be because I, the Creator, will hold your hand. And if there are folk who are disturbing your peace, I will deal with all of them and all situations that threaten your rest. Nothing is impossible for Me to do and it is I Who helps you. I got this! I am the Lord your God and you do not have to be afraid anymore. I see, I hear, I know, and I got this! (Of course, we know the Lord would not use incorrect grammar, but I paraphrased it in my interpretation to bring it home to you.)

There are many passages of assurance in the Bible, but I chose only a few to discuss with you. The next one I want to cite is Isaiah 43:1–2. It says:

1 But now thus saith the Lord that created thee, O Jacob, and He that formed thee, O Israel, Fear not: for I have redeemed thee, I have called thee by thy name; thou art mine. (*Since we are spiritual Israel, we are His. We belong to Him. And because I know I am His, I keep walking and talking for Him. I have His assurance.*)

2 When thou passest through the waters, I will be with thee; and through the rivers, they shall not overflow thee: when thou walkest through the fire, thou shalt not be burned; neither shall the flame kindle upon thee. *(This verse tells us that no matter what, He will be with us, in fact no peril can overcome us without His say so. That is some kind of assurance, isn't it? We get that same kind of assurance from Romans 8:31.)*

I told you in Lesson 3 about having to recite the 23rd Psalm by rote when I was a child, but I can tell you now that Psalm has given me hope and consolation many times in my life. I took the liberty of supplying it for you to read along with how it speaks to my soul. If you will take to reading this Psalm on a regular basis and meditating on it, you will find that you will be strengthened in your faith and perseverance.

Psalm 23

1 The Lord is my shepherd, I lack nothing. *(Everything I need, He provides and will continue to do so.)*

2 He takes me to lush pastures, He leads me to refreshing water.

3 He restores my strength. *(When I got tired, He gave me strength again.)*
He leads me down the right paths for the sake of His reputation.

4 Even when I must walk through the darkest valley, I fear no danger, for You are with me; Your rod and Your staff reassure me. *(Nope, not worried because I know that God's got this. That rod and staff are not carried for nothing.)*

5 You prepare a feast before me in plain sight of my enemies. *(In plain sight! And there was nothing they could do about it! You have defied and broken our enemies too many times for us to worry now.)*
You refresh my head with oil; my cup is completely full. *(You handled our enemies, strengthened us, and fed and watered us all at the same time. And I say, How great is our God! He is a warrior and a provider. Actually, He is all things to us!)*

6 Surely Your goodness and faithfulness will pursue me all my days, and I will live in the Lord's house for the rest of my life. *(We are like Joshua in our commitment to our God.)*

****

Psalm 46

1 God is our strong refuge; He is truly our helper in times of trouble. (*No matter from whence trouble comes the Lord God will be there to help His us.*)

2 For this reason we do not fear when the earth shakes, and the mountains tumble into the depths of the sea,

3 when its waves crash and foam, and the mountains shake before the surging sea. (Selah) (*Because we know that He is with us is the reason that you see us unshaken in our troubles. In other words, He's got this!*)

4 The river's channels bring joy to the city of God, the special, holy dwelling place of the sovereign One.

5 God lives within it, it cannot be moved. God rescues it at the break of dawn.

6 Nations are in uproar, kingdoms are overthrown. God gives a shout, the earth dissolves.

7 The Lord who commands armies is on our side! The God of Jacob is our protector! (Selah)

8 Come! Witness the exploits of the Lord, who brings devastation to the earth!

9 He brings an end to wars throughout the earth; He shatters the bow and breaks the spear; He burns the shields with fire. (*Just look at the Lord's track record. (Now you see the reason why we do not get too disturbed about situations long.)*)

10 He says, "Stop your striving and recognize that I am God! I will be exalted over the nations! I will be exalted over the earth!"

11 The Lord who commands armies is on our side! The God of Jacob is our protector! (Selah) *(This Scripture should be our battle cry of assurance in our hearts.)*

[The last two passages of Scripture came from the NET (New English Translation.) I took the liberty of inserting my own words after several verses purely for motivational purposes.]

****

As I said before:

Undeterred

The sheep have seen people come
And have seen people go
But they are not bothered overmuch
Because the Shepherd's voice they know.

****

(I hope that this treatise "I Got This" has encouraged and strengthened you. For further reading see, **Chopping My Row,** *pp 77–86.)*

As a Result

The writing you see me do and the speaking you hear me do are done from the tracks of a train that knows what it is to be derailed and to have benefited from the repairs the Master Builder has made. That is why you will hear me say this run I am making on this track of life is not all about me. It is about the depth of service I can give back to the God Who made my Momma and me. And just know that every word I pen has been given to me by the grace God has placed within me as my soul speaks to yours during these days of our mortality. I have a deeper purpose, and I work to show the world that my Momma taught me well to love, trust, and above all, to hang on to the God Who does all things well! And that is why you have seven books (including this one) already written by me and two more waiting in the wings. By the grace of God, I have come a long way or another way to say it is, *DEI Sub Numine Viget*, which means, Under God's Spirit, I Flourish.

No need to say this but just in case you don't know,
I am working hard and talking about
My God every place that I go.

So that, when I get there I am going to
Sit down and tell her how I finished writing my story
Gonna tell her how driven I was when
She left me and went on home to glory.

Gonna tell her how each subsequent step
That I took gave me joy because it brought
Me closer to that day when I could tell
Her how her teaching had made me continue
My stint of serving humanity
Then, hallelujah, Y'all, I am going to wrap
My arms around my sweet Momma
As I sing praises to God and give Him all the glory!

****

God has my attention now, and I use my life to inspire and encourage my fellowman. I do it by writing, speaking, being friendly, doing philanthropic acts, etc. I have learned through some of my troubled times that my life is not all about me. It is about learning the lessons I am taught and applying them as I live my life for Him in doing my work toward encouraging humanity.

I have learned that if you seek God daily, then your faith will grow during your trials. Can you ever have too much faith? No ma'am, you cannot. Remember, I told you that faith is priceless. *(Below is a poem I wrote to encourage a former student of mine who contacted me via social media several years after our paths had crossed. He was experiencing a broken period in his life. And yes, he is fine now, and thank you for asking. Of course, I did not use his actual name in this book. But it goes to show how the Lord will use you to help others through fiery or rainy periods in their lives.)*

There is a man named Elon
Who said that he used to be strong
Then stuff and more stuff kept hitting him hard
And he decided that he had been wrong.
But I remember a teacher who took life by the throat
And said "All right y'all, I'm making my play
Throw at me what you will and see
That I'm gonna make it anyway."
Life for me has not been a bowl of cherries
And every day has not always been merry
But the lemons I was given, I used to make lemonade
And rocked on to build a solid life
A task by which a lesser person
Would have been broken and outlaid."
About Mrs. Alma Jones, folk said that she
Was a strong lady, that there was no doubt
Many folks said that she was good and stout
When life tried to break her and often made her cry

She picked up her broken pieces and
Prayerfully laid them at Jesus' feet
And used the new batch of lemons that she had been given
To, because she was tired of lemonade,
Become skilled at making lemon pie.
So, Elon, I see in you a person such as I, in that
You get hit this way and you get hit that way
But your brain, though weary, is at all times figuring out
Ways to counteract this and maneuver around that
Even though sometimes, you get knocked down flat.
You and I have become pros at making lemonade, pie, and cake
By handling life's lemons with whatever it takes
Eating the recipes that life forces us to make
As we keep going on for posterity's sake.
We keep going on and on
Because posterity says, "We must be strong."
One last thing that I bet you didn't know
You didn't know that I admired the grit
And strength that I see in you
You are surprised, son, don't be
Because I see in you, another me!
You see, Elon, you and I were fighters
From the day that we were born
So, though you get tired and though you get worn
There is a praying old lady who
Keeps calling your name
As she lifts you up in prayer
Who asks Jesus to keep you in a fortress sturdy as a rock
To "Guard that child of hers named, Elon."
See what you did; you pulled another poem
Out of me and it was all done for you
So, don't give up fellow, you are close to breaking through
Join me in a word of prayer, one for you and one for me, too

For, yes Elon, this old teacher of yours
Still cares about what happens to you.

****

Because of broken times in my life (rainy seasons), I was able to use the writing gift God had placed within me to help a former student and several others. The suffering you go through oftentimes gets you ready for the time(s) when others may come to you in a broken and disillusioned state. What God often allows to happen is for you to be equipped with ready answers to help your fellowman. And all things that happen in your life work toward making you come forth as what? That's right, pure gold. Do you remember the Scripture that this sentence is based upon? *(Hint: It's one listed at the beginning of this lesson.)*

He Provided Meat for My Story

Liver n' Onions
What comes to your mind when I say liver and dark chocolate? Most of you probably hate the first and love the second, right? Uhm hmm, that was the reaction of my students when I used to tell them we were having liver and onions served up on our classroom menu. Most of them responded with a chorus of "Yuck!"

No, not literal liver n' onions, but it meant they were having to do expounded definitions or outlining that day. They did not like the liver and onions and when I mentioned it was good for them, they only grunted.

But by the end of the year, they were excited instead of being bothered by the mention of *liver and onions*. They knew this meant that the definitions or outlining was an automatic 100 if they put the definitions into their own words and made an *application to life*, today, or completed their outlines.

It took some thinking on their parts, at first to get their brains ready to do that level of deep thinking and it took perseverance to stick with it so they could see the good that the exercise of writing expounded definitions/outlining did for their physical bodies, which in turn, helped to build their self–concepts.

- Physical benefits: builds brain cells or dendrites.
- Intellectual benefits: expands the ability to think deeper into things that are not concrete.
- Self-esteem benefits: improves self–worth because of being more confident.

In like manner, problematic situations and trials, tribulations (rainy seasons), etc., benefit one's spiritual body because it forces one to exercise spiritual tenets such as searching the Scriptures and praying.

- Spiritual benefits: builds knowledge of the Scripture and develops stronger prayer habits,
- Faith benefits: builds a stronger faith.

Here it is: dark chocolate, which I loathe, is actually good for me. And you, too. My point? Even when things are tough and don't taste good to us and don't feel good to us in life, they may actually be for our own good. That brings back one of my favorite Scriptures, Romans 8:28, "All things work together for good for those who love the Lord."

As I told you before, everything might not be good as it is going down (happening) but it will serve to benefit us in the long run, whether dark chocolate, liver, or life!

That means to me it is all good. I just have to eat my liver and my dark chocolate because great will be the benefit/reward for doing so! Do you see what I just did? I got all that from liver and dark chocolate. Liver and dark chocolate, who would have thought?! How sweet He is!

But you know what else I gleaned from my lesson to you? I realized that back when I was still teaching school, He gave me the liver n' onions recipe idea because He knew the plans He had for me to use it in a book one day when I told my story to encourage and inspire others! He was getting me ready, even back then. W.O.W.! Who knew?!

Having said this once, I say it again for emphasis sake.
God took the storms I had gone through in my life and had me to produce a ladies' series, W.O.W. Created w.o.w., *Chopping My Row*, and now this one.

So, You Think You Are Pure Gold Now But I have a Father!

This is the reason I always tell you about prayer. There are some things, as I discovered, that you, no matter how strong you **think** you are, just cannot handle.

Several years after the death of my Momma, I got hit with a supercell of a storm! As if the first thing were not enough, I was hit with several knockout blows, this thing, and that thing, and yet another thing, and all major, mind you! I was knocked to my knees, and became a crying, crawling, and praying mess.

But I have a Father! *I am covered before and after the catastrophic happenings in my life.* I kept waiting for the feeling of peace so I would know my Father had shown, "I got this!"

I had already learned the lesson that it is often through pain that lessons are taught, and knowledge is gained, but I did not know that even after you think you have reached pure gold status in your service to Him, that life can deliver some knockout punches.

But I thank God I had savored the times He had brought me through, and I leaned my broken self on that. And I made it. So, if you are a person who is hurting and you feel like nothing ever goes right for you or that nothing ever will again, listen to me. I have been there and done that and yet, I stand before you and write to you in your agony. Here's the thing:

- As we have already said, being forced out of our comfort zones causes us to grow. Think about a lobster and how it is forced to grow. When its current shell gets so tight it must force its way out and hide under a rock to keep from being eaten by a larger animal until it grows a new one. That is not an enjoyable experience in all probability, and if a lobster could talk, it would tell you so.

- Out of need, we recognize a desire to feed. Sometimes situations come up in our lives so that we will make a move because where we are becomes uncomfortable. We realize we are not receiving what we need. This realization often causes us to reach for the Master–Feeder and His Word, the Bible. Then we feed our souls so we can make it through the turmoil in our lives. And the thing about having your soul fed from the Bible is that once it begins, you will cling to it as a lifeline because that is exactly what it is and will always be for you. Then when you make it through your rainy season, you will be willing to help someone else through theirs. You will do it out of relief that your rainy time is over, and out of a sense of paying the blessing of understanding forward just like I am doing for you.

- Rainy seasons bring much needed strength for tomorrow's journey. Yes, and as much as we hate to think about it, there will be more periods of rain in our lives. But the lesson we learned from this time will help to sustain us in other rainy seasons and further teach us to lean on the Lord, for He is faithful. And lest we forget, our leaning on Him is what He desires.

Have I had my trials, tribulations, and troubles? Yes, I have. As I said earlier, I cut my teeth on folks being jealous of me, but I never thought people would go to the lengths that some of them have. But God is in the plan, and sometimes He uses what man has determined to be your undoing to make you stronger and more adept at the job He planned for you all along, just like He did Joseph.

If you believe that God loves you, you can take some heat. You deal with the trouble and keep going just like Joseph did because you know God cares for you and that something about your adverse situation is working together for your good. (1 Peter 1:5–7; Romans 8:28)

And never feel that all is lost because I learned that with God, "All is never lost." He just does things in His own time.

The footsteps of faith from the past have charted
My course from which I have grown
And have made me into a wiser being than when I started
And have me looking toward the future…
All from the past that I've known.

In the Wee Hours of the Morn

Often when I first open my eyes to the dawn's light, thoughts of God's love flood my mind with peace. Then I am led to share that peace with my fellowman who may need to hear that God's love still abides. So, this message today is for all who are weary with traveling up and down mountains and tough terrain. This message is to let you know and/or remind you that the trouble will pass, and the sun will shine again.

As I tell you in *Chopping My Row*, all things happen for a reason. Be strengthened and know that He is ever working out things in your life. Be patient for a while longer. Things are done in God's time, not yours and not mine. Remember that and learn the lesson you were meant to learn from your current mountainous terrain. And know that you are not climbing these mountains in vain. Learn the lesson and learn it well because the time will come when you, because of your experience, will be sought out to help another soul through theirs.

And guess what? After a few such requests for advice, you will realize that God is using you!

Enjoy my poem that He has placed on my mind today because He gave it to me to give you Godspeed on your way.

Why

In the wee hours of the morn
Thoughts of God's love are born.

Thoughts that will keep me
Grounded day after day
As I help some traveler and myself
Along our appointed way.

****

(When it is over/Using My Lessons)

Pure Gold

I asked what I would have
You gave it not to me
You made me wait for better things
That you knew that my life would bring.
In Your infinite wisdom, You
Taught me how to trust
Because You knew that I needed
To develop that trust in order for me
To traverse the next leg of my journey
Into which I would soon be thrust.
For that and all the events and happenings
That have come together to make me a Woman of Faith, bold
Thank You for keeping my feet to the fire
Because in doing so, you got me prepared
For the times when life would be cold
And if I did like Momma said and

Remained pliant in your hands
I would come forth as pure gold.

****

Here, Reader, is Another Tidbit for Your Arsenal of Faith

Do you believe that God loves you? I do. And do you believe that
He always sees what is happening in the lives of His children? I
do. You, too?

Good, then let me strengthen that belief with a thought today.
Then I will give you a brief snippet of a poem and you, my
precious one, will be geared up for a day of worship, praise or
what–have–you, and folk will look at you and wonder what has
gotten into you. Some may have the temerity to even ask you
what is up with you. You can simply say, "I believe." That is all
you have to say to them, but in your heart, you will be saying, "**I
believe that if the Lord is for me, all things will work out as
He decrees they should.**" **(Romans 8:31)** That means not by
man's decree, but by God's decree.

Meant to Be

With wonder, I look back upon
The path that was laid out for me
And see that every crook and turn
That I traversed was a crook and
A turn that was meant to be.
I stand where I am and peruse
The path over which I have trod
And give grateful praise to my God
Who has given me strength to

Get Yourself Up

Follow the path ordained for me
As I turn forward and continue on my journey.
Full of determination and of hope
And knowing from my past that whatever
Situations should arise, they will be
Situations with which I can cope.
You see, shouting time is on its way
For this little nobody who loves her Lord
Blessings are forthcoming, folks and
Their arrival is heralded by precursors
Of joy, hope, and gladness to let
Me know that the calvary has been victorious
And celebrations are in order, for the day
Of victorious deliverance has come
And happiness galore has been
Handed down to stay!

If the Lord has something planned for and/or tailor–made for
you, it will be yours, bottom line, end of story!

Poetry Offerings for Lesson 4

I Believe

Folks, when you have walked through some fire,
You can stand a little heat
Because you know that the preparation of
The Lord's gospel of peace shods your feet.
You know that Your faithful Father
Is always standing by
And sees the machinations of men
Against you, before they even
Lift their hands to try.
You may be shaken
You may be rattled
But your **belief** in
God remains intact
Because of this one fact
He is faithful, so
You cannot be taken.
You know from reading your Psalms
That when your "Foot slips due
To a trap that was set for you
That He will hold you up
And that when anxious thoughts
Multiply within your mind
Delightful consolation will come behind
Your doubts and drive them away
Leaving peace where anxiety did dwell
And you will be thinking, 'I **Believe** that
God is standing by so, all is well.'"

******

Things Will Get Better

If life has taken some swings at you and you
Feel bogged down because of the battle fray
Just keep moving forward as you press on today
Because better times and crystal skies are headed your way.

****

Caught between a rock and a hard place
And I have no place to go
For I have done all that I could
So, I turn my face to my Father's throne
And watch Him handle my problems
Just because He loves me so.

****

Do You Know

Do you know
Have you heard
The news that
God provides
And walks with
Us through all
Of life's strides?

****

Cares

When I have my cares
Whether, to me, great or small
I turn them over to Jesus
And He handles them all.

****

No Fear for Me

Oh, the fury of the storm
With waves as high as can be
See the fierceness of the squall
Yet, it raises no fear in me.
The Captain of my vessel
Controls stormy winds and raging seas
Oh the fierceness of the storm
Rising winds and roaring waves
Raise no fear in me.

****

Again

He did it back then
He will do it again
Did it then
Can do it again
Then
Again
Then – again! Then again!! Then again!!!

A Better Day

"A better day begins tomorrow."
Are words that drive me when I am down and out
And my life is riddled with sorrow.

Those words have carried me when
My soul longed for better days
And I wondered if the Lord still
Guarded my steps and charted my ways.

There are times when life would
Have me feeling foolish for thinking that I could
Beat the odds that are so stacked against me
Even though, "Reaching the stars" was
What Momma often told me was my destiny.

Yet, I still hold on to the belief that God
Is the reason that I made it this far
And I believe that one day I will land on
What seems to be an unreachable star.

You see, I have been taught to make the
Best of whatever situation in which I find myself
And to deal with reality whether it brings joy or sorrow
While aiming for higher ground and remembering
That the Lord God has always shown me
That if I keep believing in and trusting Him
Things will get brighter until my gray skies are no longer dim
Because a better day begins with tomorrow.

****

Discussion Questions

1. What should Job 23:10 mean to a Christian?

_____

_____

_____

_____

2. How does 1 Peter 5:6–10 cause faith to grow?

_____

_____

_____

_____

3. Material things come and go and are not what life is all about. What Scripture supports this statement?

_Mt 6: 25 - 34 5:_

Heb 13:5   Ecc 10:11

_____

_____

4. Do Christians receive chastisement from the Lord? Why? *(Proverbs 3:12 and Hebrews 12:6, KJV)*

Love us

_____

_____

_____

5. Explain James 1:2–4.

_____

_____

_____

_____

What Do You Think?

Are Christians' enemies today afraid to bother them?

_____

_____

_____

_____

Christians are spiritual Israel. Explain this statement.

_____

_____

_____

_____

For Further Reading

Proverbs 15:3; Psalm 121:8; Psalm 94:10

Careful How You Go

Careful how you go
Lend a hand or dig a ditch
You are storing up ditches or helping hands
For yourself and your posterity, you know
They say a word to the wise is sufficient
And you can't say that I did not try to tell you so
Being kind costs you little and may gain you much
After all, the Savior taught concepts as such.
So remember, dear one, careful as you go.

****

About the Author

Alma L. Carr-Jones, a beloved educator, poet/author, a retired educator and a motivational speaker, lives in McKenzie, TN. She is a successful author of nine books to date. Alma loves to write because, as she is fond of saying, "It is something I was meant to do."

She is:

- An Avid Inspirational Daily Blog Writer grammyalmascorner.com
- A Highly Acclaimed Retired Teacher of 30 Years
- Author of Nine Books
- A Preacher's Wife of 40 years
- A w.o.w. (woman of work for the MASTER's use)

This Christian lady is one who really tries to live up to her motto of "Doing What I Can, While I Can." Since she is quite busy doing whatever her hands find to do, that old saying of *wearing out instead of rusting out* will be true of her. She says she wants to have made a difference in the lives of her fellowmen and to have built a legacy that will still speak, even after she is planted in the ground.

To have the treasure of this woman's work in your home is to have a loving dose of life as viewed from the eyes of a preacher's daughter's daughter and the wife of a preacher. This woman has a heart of gold with arms big enough and ears tender enough to help any soul stay encouraged as they make their way toward Heaven. Alma is such a jewel of a woman that she says, when you see her doing something that you admire, "Don't get it twisted; it is not me, but the glory of GOD shining through me."

Other Books by the Author

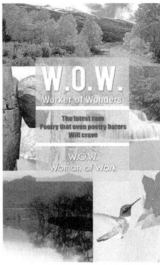

Available on Amazon and from the Author

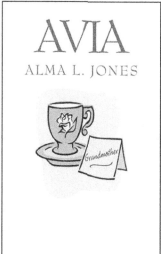

And More of
The Tallest Mountain Series
Coming Soon:

Thank you
for reading our books!

Look for other books
published by

www.TMPbooks.com

www.TMPbooks.com

*If you enjoyed this book
please remember to leave a review!*

Made in the USA
Monee, IL
19 March 2021